✤ Not Alone

✣ Mary Lewis Coakley

NOT ALONE
For The Lord Is Nigh...

THE SEABURY PRESS · NEW YORK

1981
The Seabury Press
815 Second Avenue
New York, N.Y. 10017

Library of Congress Cataloging in Publication Data

Coakley, Mary Lewis.
Not alone.
Includes bibliographical references.
1. Grief.   2. Consolation.   3. Coakley, Mary
Lewis.   I. Title.
BV4908.06   248.4   81–1803
ISBN 0-8164-2324-5   AACR2

"If I can stop one heart from breaking" by Emily Dickinson is reprinted by permission of the publishers and the Trustees of Amherst College from THE POEMS OF EMILY DICKINSON, edited by Thomas H. Johnson, Cambridge, Mass; The Belknap Press of Harvard University Press. Copyright © 1951, 1955, 1979 by The President and Fellows of Harvard College.

"When I was young, (or maybe five)" by Samuel Hoffenstein, XVIII, "Year In, You're Out," from THE COMPLETE POETRY OF SAMUEL HOFFENSTEIN is reprinted by permission of Liverite Publishing Co., W. W. Norton, copyright © 1954.

✣ Contents

✣ Part One

{1}

He was the most alive person I have ever known.

I can still hear him singing in his rich baritone voice, or laughing uproariously. I can still see him striding toward me with a grin on his face that could almost button in the back. I can still feel him throwing his arms around me and half lifting me from my feet as he whispered, "Love you, love you, love you."

I'm talking about Bill, my best friend, my confidant—my husband.

Then on that bleak November day came the cerebral hemorrage, the massive stroke, which left him comatose, utterly helpless and paralyzed, unable to move either arm or leg. When an ambulance rushed him to the Emergency Ward of Balfour Hospital, and a priest had given him the Last Rites of the Church, the nurse in attendance urged me, "Speak to him. Hearing is the last thing to go."

Obviously, she thought he had only minutes to live.

Six hours later, after our married son Joe had flown in from Nashville to Philadelphia, Bill was still alive and had been moved into the Intensive Care Unit. A nurse there explained that ordinarily the family is allowed to see ICU patients for short intervals, only every few hours, but she added, "*You* may come in oftener tonight."

Obviously, she didn't expect him to live until morning.

But come daylight he was alive! Moreover, he lived through the next day, the next night, the next day . . .

All this time my mind must have been as paralyzed as Bill's body. I don't remember clearly how I felt, but I think I half-believed that Bill and I had roles in a stage play and that every-

3

thing happening was part of our act. I do remember that later came an immense pain. I felt that I was bleeding on the inside — that my very heart had been torn out of my chest as the Aztecs tore out the pulsing hearts of living victims.

Finally, one of the doctors on the case said, "Because of the way Mr.Coakley's temperature is acting I now think he could live a week."

The week passed, and another doctor used the word I was to hear often in months ahead, "amazed." He said, "I'm amazed, but Mr. Coakley is actually better." Then he added quickly, "Not that he's out of danger. He could get an infection or pneumonia and . . ." He broke off, implying that either would be fatal.

Joe returned to Nashville, and his sweet wife, Jeanne, came up for a short stay. Bill was moved to a private room with private-duty nurses around the clock. I spent almost all day, every day, at his bedside, always hoping and waiting for the moment when Bill would open his eyes, look up, and say, "Mary."

During those days of waiting I tried to read, to write, to pray. I was too disoriented for any of these. But maybe I did pray at least with what the French call *un cri du coeur*, a cry of the heart.

I remember, too, repeating to myself as a sort of hypnotic chant, the words of the psalmist, "Our help is in the name of the Lord . . ."[1] For there seemed to be no "practical" medical help. Of the three types of strokes (an occlusion or plug in an artery, a clot in a blood vessel of the brain, and a brain hemorrhage) Bill had the most severe type, the hemorrhage, which is ordinarily fatal or, if it is not, is gravely damaging to the brain.

Several people, including the private-duty night nurse, said to me, "Try to say, 'Thy will be done,' and you'll find peace. Death might be a release for your husband and for you."

I had said, "Thy will be done," all my life in the Lord's Prayer, but to say those words *now* and to mean them was beyond me. They stuck in my throat. They might mean Bill's death and I wasn't sure I could accept that. Finally, I nerved myself to say, "Oh God, do what is best for Bill," but that too made me shudder. It too might mean death.

Well, Bill didn't die then. In fact, after the "what's best" prayer, it seemed that his condition grew a bit more stable. I calmed down enough to see, at least dimly, the alternative to death; it was a life with possibly an impaired mind, and inability to talk, to walk, to see—who knew how bad it would be? At best, if Bill should recover some of his faculties, it would mean years of tedious and perhaps painful rehabilitation for him.

"Oh God!" Those words came vocally now as a groan, as a cry, as a shout, but I didn't know exactly what I was praying for. I felt trapped between two hells. I certainly wasn't praying for Bill to die. Desperately, fiercely, I wanted him with me. Nor was I praying for him to live. A doctor-friend had said to me shortly after the CVA (as doctors call a cerebral vascular accident or stroke), "Mary, you know there are things worse than death."

Days punctuated with the two-word prayer, "Oh God," went on in slow, agonizing succession. Twenty-four days after the stroke (it seemed more like twenty-four years) Bill opened his eyes for the first time, but— "Oh God"— there was no recognition in them, no awareness. A neurologist said, "He's still in a profound coma. We call this open-eye unconsciousness a vigilant coma."

Would time bring a change?

Thanksgiving, Christmas, and New Year's Day, all went by while I, intent on Bill, scarcely noticed their passing.

But no— that's not true. I noticed Christmas because it was so brutally painful. In the morning my sister Katharine in Memphis phoned. She asked naturally enough, "How are you?" and those simple words, spoken not perfunctorily but out of real love and concern, were like a twist of the knife. Though I managed to mumble something like "Fine," I wanted to cry out, "How do you think I am? How could I possibly be anything but heartbroken and desolate?"

There was no reason in me all that day. My good friend Marie had invited me to dinner. Her grown children were there. Usually I enjoyed their company. They were attractive young people whose conversation was lively. Moreover, they were loving, sympathetic people for whom I had affection. But on that Christmas all I could think of was: How dull, stodgy, and cold they, and all other humans are, compared with Bill! I missed his special warmth, his tenderness, his joie de vivre. I hardly felt grateful for the kindness of these wonderful friends; I felt only my own vast loss. I wanted Bill and I thought: Even the best of outside friends can never, never fill the void.

I realized, too, with startling clarity, that one reason Bill and I were so close was that we could be truly frank and open with each other. I had often said to Bill over the years, "I married you because I could talk to you." And actually, I could be more completely myself with him than with anybody else I had ever known. We didn't agree about absolutely everything, but we agreed about basics so there wasn't any subject that we couldn't and didn't discuss. When we were first married, Bill dubbed himself a "heathen." He had no particular religion. He thought "that sort of thing" was OK for me, but he didn't "need it." After we had been married a couple of years, he made an about-face and turned toward faith. We began to discuss spiritual matters evening after evening, often into the wee hours. So it was that our innermost thoughts, and hopes, and beliefs which we would have been embarrassed to talk about with anybody else, were laid bare to each other. In another year Bill became a Catholic and I, not-very-deep-thinking Mary, saw my lifelong faith with new eyes. It was exciting— a shared spiritual awakening that drew us together as, I believe, nothing else could have.

No wonder everybody else seemed on the outside of our charmed circle. They were people with whom I had to heed "No Trespassing" signs. For instance, fond as I was of Marie, and as compatible as many of our interests and tastes were, we both instinctively skirted around the subject of politics, sensing that we would not have agreed on that score and that we might offend each other by too open a declaration of our views.

There it was as clear as handwriting on the wall: I would

never again have a friend as close as Bill. Without him, I could have only half-way, incomplete relationships. So that evening, sitting in Marie's comfortable living room, the Christmas tree alive with lights, a fire blazing merrily in the fireplace, her family surrounding me with their almost tangible goodwill and affection, I felt as though I were alone on the windswept steppes of Russia.

I sighed with relief when I could get away where I could let the pent-up tears flow. And they surely flowed — and flowed. I cried and sobbed so vehemently that I could hardly drive my car the short distance home. In fact, I remember that I screamed out loud like an animal in agony.

Once home, I realized that I had done an unprecedented thing: I had forgotten to open my Christmas gifts. Usually on Christmas we would open our gifts as soon as we came home from Mass. I had attended midnight Mass and had come home and gone to bed without remembering the existence of all those gaily-wrapped packages piled up so high. The next morning I had rushed off to the hospital, again oblivious of them.

Now at about 10 P.M. I began to open them. I picked up a long oblong box and out tumbled a glamorous cerise-colored robe from Jeanne and Joe. I stripped off my dress and donned it, and then the phone rang. It was Joe. He had called in the morning and now he was calling again. I was touched by his love, but I couldn't tell him how much I appreciated the second call. Everything I said tended to come out in sobs.

2

Bill continued to lie still and stiff as an Egyptian mummy. Nurses shifted his position in bed every two hours, explaining, "He'd get pneumonia or an embolism if we didn't move him."

He seemed to be blind; his eyes didn't focus properly. He could not swallow— not even his saliva; every hour or so the nurse would use a suction pump on his throat. As for nourishment, it was first supplied intravenously, and later, when the needle was removed, by gastro-nasal tube, or a tube threaded up his nose and down his throat.

Fairly soon though (I don't remember how long after the CVA) a doctor told me, "We're going to get Mr.Coakley out of bed. If he lies prone indefinitely, he won't last much longer."

Since Bill was a deadweight and a rather big man, it took five nurses to lift him, one at the head, and two on each side. They used to joke about "mustering the troops" for this daily feat.

Once they had him up, they tied him in a chair, put sandbags at his feet to keep him from sliding forward, and towels at his neck to keep his head from lolling.

Orderlies even occasionally put him on a wheeled stretcher and took him to the PT (Physical Therapy) department where they transferred him to a tilt-board, strapped him on, and raised him mechanically to an almost vertical position. The procedure supposedly aided circulation.

About this time, the private-duty afternoon nurse suggested that I get canvas gym shoes for Bill to wear in bed off and on, explaining that they would prevent his toes from curling under permanently. I bought them that very day.

It was during the Christmas holidays that my oldest grandchild, a teenager, flew up from Tennessee to be with me for a few days and it was she who made the first hopeful statement that anybody had made since the stroke. I was leaning over Bill and telling him, "Honey, this is your favorite wife" (one of his nicknames for me), and she said, "Oh Grand-Mary, you don't have to tell him who you are. He knows."

How devoutly I hoped she was right! He gave no sign that he did.

Sometime after my granddaughter left, my sister Katharine from Memphis came up for a visit. She urged me to get back to my writing. In that far-off prestroke life, I had been a free-lance writer with a number of books, magazine articles, and newspaper stories to my credit. But to resume writing seemed to me preposterous. I couldn't think of anything but Bill. Besides, how could I write without him? I needed his backing. Every time I sold a piece, even to an obscure magazine, he was likely to boast to our friends, "Mary's done it again!" To write without him at hand would be like our Little Theatre group, The Wyncote Players, putting on a show without an audience to appreciate and applaud its efforts.

Also, Bill was my critic. I hated to send anything to an editor until he had read it because often he gave me invaluable comment. I didn't always like it at first when he said, "You belabored this point," or "Why don't you develop this point more?" but usually I'd see that he was right. Just the day before the stroke, I had written a letter to an editor, proposing an article. I ended it quite cleverly— I thought. I showed the letter to Bill. His comment was, "I'd say for the bulk of the letter, OK; for the ending, ugh. The ending is cutesy and contrived."

I walked off practically in a huff, but then I reread the letter and I saw what he meant. I put it aside, intending to revamp it and send it out later. Because of the stroke I never did of course.

Katharine probably couldn't understand why I started to cry when she said, "Try to get back to your writing."

It was during her visit that Bill first stirred; he moved his right hand. Incidentally, that caused the doctors to change their opinion on one point. Although the paralysis was bilateral, they had thought it more pronounced on the right side; now they said it was more pronounced on the left.

Moreover, I think it was during her visit that Bill first moved his lips and other facial muscles, though he never smiled, or frowned, or raised his eyebrows, or winked, or showed any recognizable emotion. (In prestroke days he had been good at pantomime, and he, more than I, had been active in our Little Theatre group.) Now it was impossible to gauge if anything at all was going on in his mind. Indeed, I couldn't tell about certain aspects of his physical state. Just in case he had not lost his eyesight, I sometimes put his glasses on him and I sensed he wanted me to. Then one day my heart nearly stopped beating. As I put on the glasses, he kissed my hand.

Katharine was in the room at the time, but I felt that I couldn't express how I felt to anybody without exploding into laughter, or sobs, or generally having hysterics. I ran out of the door to the hall and leaned up against the wall like a limp rag doll.

The kiss was not repeated for weeks. But on another day when I was alone with Bill his eyes met mine and I had a strong, sure feeling that he knew me and was responding by his gaze to my "I love you." Something definitely passed between us. Afterwards a wave of happiness engulfed me and a strange feeling of awe as though we were communicating over a mystic gulf.

Only the day before as I said the "Morning Offering" prayer, the one that goes, "Oh Jesus . . . I offer you all the prayers, works, joys, and sufferings of this day . . ." I had thought: I should omit the word "joys." I had told myself: There are no joys now. That day when I knew that Bill knew me and was telling me silently that he loved me as always, I felt joy— great exultant joy.

It is strange that during the agonizing period of Bill's illness when I felt literally crushed with sorrow, came some of the happiest moments of my life. The lows were lower than outsiders could possibly imagine, but the highs were higher. They carried me to another realm seemingly above this familiar planet, Earth.

That precious moment passed and during the next weeks Bill was incommunicado. Moreover, he had physical setbacks with three distinct crises. To expect him to come through any one of them alive was like expecting a man to make it across a tight-rope strung between two skyscrapers one hundred stories above Fifth Avenue. Bill performed the feat.

The last crisis was on a Sunday when hospital personnel is minimal, and doctors seem to be nonexistent. Bill's tempera-ture shot up and I thought he was dying. Neither the nurses nor I could locate a doctor by phone, and the head floor nurse was having difficulty getting the intern; he was, she said, with another dying patient. I picked up the phone about to call Joe and say, "This is it," but instead I thought of calling our doctor-friend, Frank (an obstetrician-gynecologist who, of course, had not been on the case) hoping he could do something.

Kind as always, he came right over and brought the resident doctor into the room. The latter ordered that Bill be put back on intravenous fluids to increase the liquids in his body and gave him some shots.

That "severe respiratory infection," as the resident called it, cleared up and one of Bill's doctors said to me, "Another close call! This man is amazing."

On days when there was no physical crisis for Bill, it seems there were emotional ones for me. I remember the shock and horror I felt when I first heard two doctors discussing "brain damage" in "*both* brain-hemispheres." Somehow I had taken comfort in the thought that perhaps one hemisphere was intact, and since a person purportedly uses only part of the brain any-how, I hoped (if I didn't exactly think) that Bill might have enough sound gray-matter to function. And as a dog grabs at a bone, I had eagerly grasped at a remark of one friend, "Bill with half a brain would still have a higher I.Q. than most of us with the whole bit."

Another emotional crisis came for me when a friend who

found me crying said, "Oh, I know it's awful to see Bill as he is, a human vegetable, but he can't last much longer."

She had actually meant to be consoling! But I felt an almost physical revulsion at her words. First of all, I wanted Bill to "last much longer." Then certainly he wasn't a vegetable! He was a magnificent human being and always would be.

Another emotional crisis came the day a friend said to me soothingly, "Well, if people have one stroke, they nearly always have another that takes them off quickly."

She, too, had meant to be consoling. But I hadn't thought of the possibility of another stroke and when her words alerted me to it, I was filled with fear and dread.

An acute emotional crisis came the day I asked a doctor-friend (not on the case) when or if Bill would recover his speech. He said frankly, "Since the damage now seems to be more on the left side, the chance of Bill's ever speaking again are almost nil."

Though my immediate reaction was disbelief, in the middle of the night those words came back to send an icy wind of fear into my very bones. I thrashed around in bed and cried out loud, "Oh God, no!"

Then came the thought: When Bill regains consciousness will he try to speak to me? How can I break the news to him that he has lost the power to speak? I agonized over that for a long while.

I was upset (though in far lesser degree) when I learned that the hospital would not keep Bill. A kind friend (whose wife had died some months before) tried to tell me that hospitals keep only two types of patients, those who may die any day, and those who can recover. The patient who is going to be ill and helpless for an indefinite period, that is, the chronically ill patient, must leave. I didn't take in what he was saying. I suppose there is a limit to the anxiety that can crowd into the mind at one time. But I did understand the facts when one of Bill's doctors told them to me and explained, "This hospital rarely keeps a patient as long as it has already kept Mr. Coakley— it's been ten weeks— and the only reason was that we couldn't move him. It wouldn't have been safe before this."

I didn't want Bill to go to a regular nursing home. I desperately wanted him to go to one of the big, Philadelphia-area rehabilitation centers where he'd get therapy to restore leg and arm motion. Though this particular doctor was the most optimistic of the four doctors on he case, he was not encouraging about therapy. He said, "There's so little that Mr.Coakley can take."

"Do you see him then as permanently bedridden?" I asked.

"If there's any improvement, the day may come when you and/or another person will be able to stand him and transfer him from bed to wheelchair. That's the *most* we can expect."

As for getting Bill into one of the big rehab centers, the doctor said, "No use trying. I can't ask any of them to send a therapist out here to evaluate Mr.Coakley when I know beforehand they wouldn't accept him."

I insisted I wanted therapy for Bill so finally the doctor said, "Your best bet is probably Green Valley Hospital. That's a combination hospital, nursing home, and rehab center. If it refuses him, you'll have to look for a regular nursing home. Some of them have a resident therapist."

A doctor-friend of ours (not connected with Bill's case) knew a doctor on the Green Valley staff. Maybe the good word he put in for us there helped. Anyway, Bill was admitted — and without prior evaluation.

I rode over in the ambulance with him and I'll never forget my introduction to the place. The Doctor-Director, after examining Bill, called me into his office. For a moment, as I sat facing him across his shiny desk, he was silent, so I was on the point of initiating the conversation by asking about therapy for Bill. I never got the words out; I was struck dumb by the doctor's words to me. He said, "I wish I could tell you that your husband would die tonight, but he could live indefinitely."

All I could do was gasp. It seemed utterly incredible that a doctor could talk in that vein. Then it seemed extremely imperceptive. I didn't want Bill to die. Oh dear Lord, no, no, no! I wanted him to live.

As I left Green Valley on that bitterly cold, gray February

evening, I walked up the driveway with the cry on my lips, "My God, my God, why hast Thou forsaken me?"[1]

It seems theatrical as I think back on it now, but the words came spontaneously and were totally sincere. I felt that God had forsaken and forgotten Bill and me.

Some solace came to me next morning when I asked myself: Does it have to be either death or continued helplessness and stupor? God could cure Bill. "Is there anything hard to God?"[2]

Of course a cure would be a miracle, but so what? My friend, Therese, a month or more before when Bill's life hung on a thread, had said, "Pray for a *cure*," and she added, "Ask Our Lady's intercession." The very first miracle recorded in the Gospels as performed by Jesus came after Mary told her Son at the Cana wedding, "They have no wine." Sure that He would act, once He understood the need, she had instructed the waiters, ". . . Whatsoever he shall say to you, do ye."[3]

Actually, I had tried even then to pray as Therese suggested and when the Balfour doctor told me that he saw nothing ahead for Bill but bed and wheelchair, I had answered, "If medical art is impotent, I'll have to pray for a miracle."

He had replied, "You've already had a miracle. This man shouldn't be alive."

Now I asked myself, if one miracle, why not two? The trouble was that I didn't deserve a miracle— not me. Well, the miracle would be for Bill. He deserved— no, he didn't *deserve* one. No human being ever really deserves a miracle. We receive them because God is gracious. Every Christian believes that God became man for him and that act, that event, the Incarnation, was miraculous.

My prayer for the Bill-miracle didn't use many words. It was often no more than a looking toward God with an unspoken plea, "Help!" I was conscious that He was there with me in the dark.

"In the dark!" I felt as though I were groping my way along a dark tunnel deep in the earth. No light penetrated it. I could not see the end of the tunnel, but I clung to the belief that there had to be one. And maybe, though I didn't realize it at the time, it was a kind of miracle that after nearly three months, and after every doctor on the case had given a prognosis of helpless and hopeless, I was able to hope and to think more seriously than ever of a cure. I had no encouragement. No relative or friend except Therese mentioned the possibility of a cure. Yet I now began to hope for, to pray for, and to half-expect one.

Or was it natural enough that after being initially thrown into shock by seeing strong, vigorous, highly intelligent Bill reduced to helplessness and mindlessness, I was now coming to, as it were, and rallying my forces to fight back in the only way possible? When there is no natural remedy for a situation, a person has to turn to the supernatural or give up. My sister in California who is a nun (when I phoned her the day of the stroke saying, "The doctors give me no hope. All we can do is pray") had said, "But prayer is the important thing."

Yes, I hoped and prayed now for a miraculous cure and the Doctor-Director must have sensed this new hope or this escape into fantasy as he, no doubt, would have called it, for he said to me, "The kindest thing I can do for you is to help you face reality. All indications are that Mr. Coakley will never be any different than he is today."

"I can understand what you're saying with my mind," I answered, "but there's a part of me that cannot accept it. If I accepted it, I'd have to say, 'He might as well be dead.'"

"I can say plainly that he would be *better* off dead," the doctor replied, "but you must at least try to accept the facts and be content with giving your husband good care."

I wasn't "content." And "reality?" I asked myself: What's that? God is real and He is almighty. There are so-called "miracles of science" all the time. And who is the ultimate source of these miracles if not God? After all, it is His world and His creation. He could either lead some man to discover a remedy for damaged brain cells, or He could act directly. He is omnipotent. I believe that — or don't I?

At times I wasn't sure what I believed, so along with my prayers for Bill's cure, I said as had the man in the Gospels, "I do believe, Lord: help my unbelief."[4]

3

In prestroke days Bill had always been protective, and he would say laughingly, "It's my job to cherish you. If I can't cherish my own wife, whose wife can I cherish?"

Definitely, he did cherish me and far beyond his oft-repeated formula of "bring roses and wine early and often, serve her coffee in bed on Sunday mornings, and do those household chores that need a strong back and a weak mind."

So, early in his illness the idea struck me that the best way I could convince Bill that he must hang in there and fight his illness, was to tell him, "I need you, so you've got to get well."

There was no sign that he heard me, but just in case he did, I went on making my little speech practically every hour on the hour.

One of the private-duty nurses took me to task. She said, "You shouldn't talk that way to Mr. Coakley. He can't die because you won't let him."

That was exactly the idea! Naturally her words encouraged me to go on. And I could not accept the hopeless prognosis. I told Joe, who flew up that first weekend Bill was in Green Valley, "The therapy here has got to change things," and inwardly I added: It will be the tool that God uses for a miracle.

But soon after Joe left town, I saw that the Director was scheduling almost no therapy for Bill.

A cerebral hemorrhage does not damage muscles as polio does; they remain as healthy as ever. The hemorrhage affects brain cells and since some of these cells should direct muscles, the muscles become useless when the cells are too damaged to give direction. The hemorrhage suffuses the brain with blood and later as the blood recedes, it leaves some brain cells utterly destroyed, while others, only temporarily knocked out, are capable of recovering function. Usually there is more damage on one side of the brain than on the other, so that a stroke victim has more paralysis on one side of his body. But to prod even the less affected side (from which hopefully the blood has receded) to work again, the stimulus of passive exercises helps.

I was heartsick when the Green Valley speech-therapist told me bluntly, "I can't work with Mr. Coakley."

Really the only therapy Bill received was electrical stimulation of throat muscles and the doctor didn't promise much from that. He said, "It won't restore swallowing power. It will merely keep the muscles from atrophying so that if the brain were ever again to direct them, they will be able to respond."

Remembering Balfour's therapy, I asked, "Why not at least put my husband on the tilt-board? Is his heart too weak to stand it? Or do you think therapy of that kind might precipitate another stroke?"

"Our tests give no indication of anything wrong with Mr. Coakley's heart," the doctor answered. "As for another stroke, anybody who has had one stroke is likely to have others. But I don't think therapy would necessarily increase the danger."

"Why not stand him between two therapists then?" I asked. "That might get things started. I saw stroke-patients being stood up in Balfour."

"We tried to stand Mr. Coakley, but he has to be held up. He can do absolutely nothing on his own. He can't help himself in the smallest way. If we sit him up in bed, he falls over. The part of the brain that controls motion is gone."

After a slight pause, he added, "No therapist can give your husband what he does not have. It will do no good to stand him if he can't eventually help himself and that, I'm sure, he cannot do."

A few weeks went by and then the Director called me into his office and said as he had before, "The kindest thing I can do for you is help you face facts. Motion-recovery, if it comes, usually comes within three or four months. Mr. Coakley does not move at all. Neither my colleagues here, nor myself, see any hope that he will ever walk or talk again. I'm taking him from the rehab unit and putting him in the nursing-care unit.

I felt as though he had lashed out at me with a whip. I staggered from the room unable at the moment even to argue back. Where was the cure? Things were worse, not better.

That night the now-familiar fears swarmed into my mind like a horde of locusts. Would Bill ever regain full consciousness? Would he ever again recognize me? It seemed the greatest of tragedies that Bill—alert, vibrant Bill—should be like this forever.

Then came secondary fears. Would I run out of money to care for him properly? He had to have the best. Our Major Medical insurance policy had covered most of his expenses until now, but would it do that when he was moved into the nursing-unit? The "fine print," which I had tried to read carefully, seemed to say that the policy covered hospital, not nursing-home, expenses.

Besides, the policy had a monetary limit. If Bill were never to receive therapy and were always to lie helpless in bed, he would continue to need nursing care for . . . years?? At Balfour I had had private-duty nurses for him around the clock. At Green Valley, the Director had insisted that I have at least two shifts, and the cost of those sixteen hours a day was— well, it was monstrous. It ran into thousands per month. If Bill's nursing care stretched beyond months into years, we would overtake the limit and then, paying everything from our own pockets, we would use up everything we had, and what of Bill then? Would he land in some public institution?

That night, lying awake and frightened, my mind spun around like a toy top. I could sell the house with most of its contents and get a tiny apartment. That would mean no real estate taxes, no fuel bills, no upkeep. Then too, I'd have the money from the sale to invest for extra income. But if a move, why not a move to Nashville where I'd be near Joe and Jeanne? I could get an ambulance to take Bill to the airport, (What provision did airlines make for a passenger who couldn't sit up?) and Joe could arrange for an ambulance to meet Bill at the Nashville airport and take him to some nursing home. But what a project!

Oh, what was best?

At long last, as the first faint light of dawn appeared in the sky I prayed, "Oh God, You've got to take over. I can't cope."

Unconsciously, I was following Bill's prestroke formula. He used to repeat the slogan, "Let go, and let God," and say, "Sooner or later we all have to make our Declaration of *De*pendence on God. If we're dependent on God, we can be independent of our own weakness."

At 9 A.M. I phoned the insurance company and asked what the policy covered. The voice on the other end of the wire said, "Since Green Valley is a hospital as well as a nursing home, the policy will cover expenses as long as Mr. Coakley is in any part of the place."

My sigh of relief was long and loud.

Although using the insurance money would hasten the day when it would run out, the immediate problem was solved. I wouldn't have to take any drastic steps— yet. Temporarily then, I could push finances to the back-burner and concentrate on getting more therapy for Bill. "First things first."

I tried to pray for guidance. Prayer was hard for me. Often I would pick up a prayer book and read, but the words might have been written in Greek or Aramaic. When I reached the end of a page, I didn't know what I had read. Nor could I pray in my own words except in short snatches; my skittish mind would dart off to some problem.

My best prayer-attempt was the rosary. It kept my jittery mind on course for a longer time because it had a pattern to follow and the mental pictures I conjured up as I tried to think of the "Mysteries" or the events of Christ's life, helped me link prayerful thoughts together like stitches on a knitting needle.

When I began, "I believe in God," the words bolstered my faith. There were times when I didn't know whether I had lost my faith. Then the words, "Father Almighty" helped; they reminded me that God could do anything. I liked especially the word to the Virgin, "Pray for us sinners *NOW*!" Never, I felt, were Bill and I in greater need than now at this very instant.

In fact, when I couldn't say the rosary, I often said just the "now" phrase. Driving back and forth to Green Valley the phrase became my theme song; it haunted my mind like notes from a musical score that I couldn't banish if I wanted to.

Then just holding the rosary was a psychological help. I remember some nights getting home so emotionally spent and physically tired that I felt I could hardly drag myself up the stairs; then when I finally fell into bed I certainly couldn't say long prayers, but I could reach for my rosary and its chain was like a tangible lifeline to cling to.

Woven through the Green Valley days was the rosary. The words, perhaps *because* they were repetitious, acted as a tranquilizer. I didn't, I couldn't, always think of their exact meaning, but they were my way of saying, "God help us! God help us! Oh dear God, please, please, please help us!"

The prayers of other people were a big thing, too, in this Green Valley period. They came from all sides — from family, friends, and acquaintances. The prayers of my sister-in-the-convent were as constant as a vigil light. Then a nun in a local convent assured me that she prayed daily for Bill as did her "Sisters." Every single Sunday in our parish church there was public mention of Bill to which the congregation responded, "Lord, hear our prayer." Therese not only prayed herself but she asked the prayers of a little group she belonged to. Marie's son came to the hospital several times with some young men his age to say the rosary kneeling at Bill's bedside. Another friend, Bea B., (incidentally the person through whom I met Therese) came over one evening with Mass cards showing that she and many other friends had had Masses said for Bill. Two of the girls in Bill's office sent a prayer-card literally every week. My next door neighbor, Deana, asked her Baptist church members to pray for Bill as did another Baptist friend in Memphis. Other dear friends like Alberta and Phil, Ruth and Frank, Anne and

Ray, Betty and ... and ... all assured me that they were praying for Bill.

Then about this time I wrote a personal letter to the editor of a small Catholic newspaper and asked him to pray for Bill. I was surprised when he printed my letter and moreover passed it on to another editor of another Catholic paper who also printed it. When those letters appeared there came an avalanche; I began hearing from people in just about every state in the Union and a few from Canada. All promised prayers for Bill.

With this storming of Heaven, was it "unrealistic" to keep hoping for a miracle? And I told myself: In prayer, everybody asks for a miracle in the sense that he or she asks God to intervene in the ordinary course of events. He doesn't always ask God to suspend or deflect the laws of Nature, but he does ask divine intervention. If he is praying for a raise in salary, or a promotion, he is asking God to give affairs a push in a certain direction. Without that push, he fears he might not get what he wants. Certainly, if God is God, that is if He is an Omnipotent Being, then it's just as easy for Him to give a big push as to give a little one.

Therese mentioned May thirteenth, the day the Blessed Mother first appeared in Fatima, as a sort of target date, a day on which I might receive an answer to prayer— a miracle?

My reaction was shock! May! With each day seeming to me like a month— no a year— May seemed far, far off in some misty, unreal future. To wait for it would be waiting for the millenium. I could hardly believe that Bill (or I for that matter) would still be alive *that* long unless some dramatic progress came soon. We couldn't go on like this. How could we get through the next day or the next hour?

I didn't mark with a red crayon or paste with a gold star the date on which something did happen, but probably only a month later, and long before May thirteenth, came an event so BIG, so awesome, that even today it gives me goose pimples to recall it. I was sitting by Bill's bed one afternoon and the covers seemed to move ever so slightly. Was it an optical illusion? I edged forward on my chair hardly daring to breathe. Yes, he was moving his leg. It was like seeing the dead arise. It filled me with the awe of Easter morning.

I ran to the Doctor-Director with the news. He was skeptical but he agreed to go back to Bill's room with me. I pulled down Bill's covers, tapped his right leg and he moved it.

He did! He did! What's more he moved it farther than I myself expected or believed he could. The staid doctor actually exclaimed what sounded like, "Well, I be damned," and then more clearly he said, "That's fabulous."

In a day or so he reversed his opinion about therapy for Bill saying, "We'll try it."

4

Now the gates were open!

Therapists used the pulley exercises on Bill's right arm, they put him on a table and moved his legs, but — that was all. I couldn't understand why they didn't do more. I wanted them to try everything in the book. When I said so to one of the private-duty nurses, Anna, she answered, "You should see the head therapist at St.Thomas Hospital, Dominic Cardelli.* He tries everything."

"What does he do?" I asked.

She explained that he used "strenuous methods," and he had done "wonders for patients," even those labelled "hopeless." She mentioned one particular "hopeless" man and said, "I nursed him, and Mr.Cardelli finally taught him to walk with some support from his wife and with the use of a cane, of course."

I had a friend, Bea C. (not the Bea B. mentioned earlier) who had a responsible position at St.Thomas. I phoned her pronto. She confirmed what Anna had said and called Mr.Cardelli "a wizard." In fact, she said, "I almost think he hypnotizes people, but he gets results."

I also phoned another friend who was on the Board of Directors at St.Thomas. He declared, "If Bill is ever going to walk again, this fellow Cardelli is the man who can make him do it."

Then I dug up some former patients of Mr.Cardelli, and phoned them or their families.

Obviously, there was only one thing left; I had to see Mr.Cardelli myself. I called and made an appointment.

*He now has his own clinic.

When I arrived at St. Thomas Hospital, a therapist ushered me into a rather bare antiseptic-looking waiting room. Then Mr. Cardelli came in, and it was as though his presence set the place ablaze, for suddenly the atmosphere was crackling. He seemed awesomely big, not only because he was built like a full-back, but big because his aura filled the room. He strode toward me, his hand outstretched to grip mine. He didn't bother with "How do you do?" or even "Good afternoon." His first words to me were, "I want to help your husband."

I almost jumped out of my shoes, I was so startled. Everybody else — doctors, therapists, and nurses — had said openly or had hinted, "There's nothing we can do for your husband but keep him comfortable."

I blurted out Bill's story, the words tumbling over one another as I talked. Mr. Cardelli leaned toward me and his piercing blue eyes never left my face. Maybe vaguely I glimpsed what my friend Bea had meant when she said, "I almost think he hypnotizes people." He seemed to have the zeal of an Old Testament prophet and the dedication of a St. Francis. He told me, "No doctor can declare a patient hopeless. Only time and God can show what a patient can do."

"But my husband can't even swallow and he can't talk," I repeated to make sure he understood the gravity of the case.

He repeated his thought too, "Doctors aren't infallible. They know there's brain damage, but they can't know its exact extent. The brain is too complex. I'd stop working with a patient only if the good Lord Himself proved the man hopeless. The first thing is to get Mr. Coakley on his feet. Everything else comes later. If Mr. Coakley takes a few steps even with lots of help that will improve his circulation which in turn will affect everything, even his chances of speaking again."

Before I left St. Thomas Hospital that day, I asked Mr. Cardelli to come to Green Valley to evaluate Bill.

A bright ray of light was penetrating the tunnel. It was, I felt, another installment on the miracle and later I said as much to nurse Anna.

Instead of rejoicing with me, she answered, "Of course you know that if Mr. Coakley should ever regain any self-motion, his mind will remain the same. It won't have its former powers. Mr. Coakley will never be able to read or to follow a logical line of reasoning, and he may have lost his eyesight."

It was comical the way everybody but Mr. Cardelli felt it necessary to douse my hopes but, like Queen Victoria, I was not amused. I thought the view of these would-be "realists" was narrow. It reminded me of the three blind men who examined the elephant. The first man felt the animal's trunk and said, "An elephant is like a tree." The second felt the animal's body and said, "An elephant is like a wall." The third felt the animal's tail and said, "An elephant is like a rope." The realists, I agreed, were right as far as they went; they saw Bill's disabilities. But they didn't see the picture as a whole. They didn't take into account God's help which was limitless. They didn't take into account Bill's spirit which had always been as determined as that of any human being I had ever known.

After I left Anna I went to see the Director expecting similar discouraging words from him. But when I told him that I would like to consult an outside therapist, he surprised me by taking another tack; he became angry. He considered my request an affront to himself and to his staff of therapists and he said, "I will not allow an outside therapist to set foot in this hospital much less examine Mr. Coakley. You cannot equate the opinion of any therapist with that of a doctor. He's scarcely more than a nurse."

I tried to think of a placating answer, but before I had, the doctor said in a calmer voice, "Let me call in a neurologist for a consultation."

That evening I phoned Joe and talked over the suggestion with him. He said, "Since Cardelli says one thing, the Director another, it's sensible to get a third opinion from a consultant. You'll never be satisfied to let the matter drop. If the consultant OKs therapy you can still make the move to St. Thomas and to Cardelli."

I would have preferred to skip the consultation and take Bill to St. Thomas right off but I didn't know exactly how to swing it, so reluctantly I followed Joe's advice and told the Director to call in a neurologist.

A day or two before the supposedly eminent specialist was to see Bill, the Green Valley therapists put Bill's legs in canvas splints so that his knees wouldn't buckle and stood him between them.

When I found this out, I ran to the phone and called Cardelli to tell him the good news. He said, "Maybe you prodded them into action with your talk of more extensive therapy here. But who cares why they did what they did? They did it and that's good. It doesn't matter where Mr. Coakley gets therapy as long as he gets it." Then he added, "If he ever comes here, I'll go further. I'll walk him."

Walk him? I didn't know what Mr. Cardelli meant. "Come over this afternoon about 2:30 and I'll show you," he said.

When I went, I saw orderlies bring a nineteen-year-old girl into the PT Room on a wheeled stretcher. She had suffered brain damage in an automobile accident and apparently was still comatose.

Mr. Cardelli and one of his aides got her to her feet and propped her up between them. Then they stooped low enough to pull her arms around their necks. Her eyes were closed, her mouth hung open, and she drooled. But they "walked" her by leaning over and lifting her feet for her, one after the other. Close behind her came a third therapist with his hands behind her ears holding up her head that otherwise would have lolled, and behind him came a fourth pushing a wheelchair ready for the signal to seat her. In front of her, went a fifth therapist carrying the girl's catheter bag.

For Cardelli and his teammate who lifted her feet, the constant stooping must have been backbreaking. I never saw therapists at Green Valley or any place else, work *that* hard.

I was psychologically ready to move Bill to St. Thomas right then but, having made the consultation commitment, I had to wait.

On one of the days of waiting when I stopped at church *en*

route to Green Valley, I saw a woman on crutches in the congregation, and I felt a fierce and fiery pang of envy. If only Bill could walk with crutches! Since I couldn't get him to Cardelli, and the consultant was in no hurry to come, crutches seemed at that moment a too-much-to-be-hoped-for dream. But one passage from the Psalms in the Mass was, "The right hand of the Lord hath wrought strength . . . . I shall not die, but live: and shall declare the works of the Lord."[1]

As I often did in those days, I took a pencil and notebook from my purse and jotted down the verses that gave me comfort, thinking as I wrote: If Bill is cured or ever gets as far as walking with crutches I will declare the works of the Lord by tongue and typewriter.

Therese was always talking about Our Lady of Fatima. The Blessed Mother when she appeared in 1917 to the three children in the Portuguese village of Fatima had asked for prayers for peace and for Russia's conversion from Communism. She said that unless "enough people" prayed, Communism would spread throughout the world. If Bill were cured through her intercession (and I pleaded for it every day and almost every waking hour), that would be one small item to help publicize her message.

The thought probably helped me bridge the gap until the consultant arrived. I decided that if he said Bill was capable of more therapy, the Nazareth move was a must. If he said Bill was incapable of therapy— well, I would still move Bill to St. Thomas because, no matter how long the odds, I would have nothing to lose by taking the gamble.

What I actually expected was an indefinite, in-between verdict.

Then the verdict came! It was something I had never thought of. The consultant said in effect, "Further therapy will kill your husband."

Kill! I was aghast! I couldn't kill Bill. All my plans about Cardelli came crashing down around my head. I would have to let Bill lie in bed forever. How the old vigorous Bill would have hated that! Did the poststroke Bill understand his helplessness?

As these thoughts raced through my head I only half heard

the doctor's explanation, "There might be further CVAs if Mr. Coakley is not handled carefully. Strenuous therapy could raise his blood pressure because he will try to do something he is completely incapable of doing and that will frustrate him."

I was so stunned that I didn't remember till afterwards that the Director had once given a contrary opinion: he had said that therapy would not necessarily increase the danger of additional CVAs. His only reason for vetoing further theraphy for Bill was its uselessness.

With effort I did pull myself together enough to ask the consultant a few more questions. Maybe I would not have been able to do that if I hadn't made notes beforehand. I asked, "Is there any hope that at some future date my husband can take therapy and learn to walk?"

The doctor gave me an SOS (Same Old Stuff) answer about damage to the stem of the brain ruling out walking now and forever.

Clutching at straws I said, "I've read that we use only a fraction of our brains, so if one part collapses, another part often takes over. Couldn't that happen here?"

The consultant answered, "The thinking part of Mr. Coakley's brain probably has considerable function left. It's the motor part that is damaged."

My eyes popped open. Here was a new angle! I realized that I had subconsciously assumed that the physical powers of walking and talking had to make a comeback before his mental wheels would again turn in anything like a normal manner. Now, looking at the picture from another vantage point, I asked, "If he thinks with any clarity, does that mean there's more hope that he'll regain his speech?"

"Oh, no," came the answer; speech is gone with the wind.

Then I remembered that while Bill was still in Balfour, the night-nurse had told me that Bill had spoken three words. I don't know why I didn't attach more importance to that glad news at the time. It had cheered me of course, but I was then so desperately concerned with his living from one hour to the next, that I pushed everything else to the back-burner. When I told the consultant about the words, he replied, "It's possible that the nurse did hear him speak. These vascular conditions are progressive. I suspect that since the cerebral aneurysm of five months ago, Mr.Coakley has had minute vascular accidents that were not recognized as such."

To my next question asking how much of his condition Bill understood, he answered, "No one can determine that. But I have the impression of an active, keen mind there."

"If I read to him would he understand?"

"Umm . . . possibly."

"Will he ever be able to read to himself?"

"Oh no," the doctor answered. "He can see to a limited extent, but his eyes don't move normally."

The last question I had was about Mr.Cardelli's theory, "Would standing my husband and trying to make him walk improve his circulation and so indirectly help some of his other conditions?"

"It would help the functioning of his internal organs," the consultant replied. "However, since walking depends on brain function, it wouldn't help him to walk again by himself."

If I had been low before the consultation, I was lower afterwards. I couldn't give Bill therapy. I couldn't do anything for him. I was stymied.

That night my friend Marie came over with food and fixed me dinner. I've heard about people crying in their beer; I cried in the clam chowder we ate.

After she left, I tried to pray but no words came. A gesture was all I could manage. Lying face downward on the bed, I flung out my right hand as though I were reaching for the sustaining hand of God.

{5}

The day after the consultation I felt so leaden with sorrow and disappointment that my very body seemed unbearably heavy. When I arrived at Green Valley Hospital, Anna must have sensed how I felt for she seemed very sympathetic. She said, "There's danger of further CVAs, therapy or no." Then she went on about Mr. Cardelli's patient whom she had nursed, saying, "In a way he was worse off than Mr. Coakley because he had a weak heart along with his other troubles, yet he learned to walk."

This sounded as though she were encouraging me to forget the consultant's warning about killing Bill. What could I believe?

I stewed over the question all day, and when I got home that evening, I made a few phone calls to get other opinions. Our doctor-friend, Frank, said, "Yes, extensive therapy might precipitate a certain kind of stroke, but lying in bed could precipitate another kind, the kind caused by an embolism. It's Risk A against Risk B."

Bea agreed and she added, "I've never heard of a patient that Cardelli worked with having a CVA because of therapy. I think he's a careful, conscientious man."

Jack (Bea's husband) on the upstairs extension chimed in, "If I were in Bill's place, I'd opt for the extra therapy, risk or no risk, and you know darn well Bill would do the same."

In gathering my little nosegay of opinions, I didn't overlook our pastor. From the beginning he had listened to and counselled me in all my worries and problems. When I told him the fear about killing Bill, he said practically the same thing that the others had said and I responded, "I'll think it over and maybe approach Mr. Cardelli again."

"Yes," said the priest, "think it over and pray for guidance. Then give yourself a deadline to decide. When the deadline comes, do whatever you think is best. It will be the right thing."

I took his advice and said to myself: March twenty-fifth, the feast of the Annunciation (when the angel Gabriel told the Blessed Virgin, ". . . thou hast found grace with God. Behold thou shalt conceive in thy womb, and shalt bring forth a son; and thou shalt call his name Jesus."[1]) would be D–Day, Decision Day.

Meantime, one morning I woke up and found a thought as vivid as though it were written in neon lights in Times Square flashing across my mind: That consultant is wrong! He's wrong about therapy killing Bill! In fact, I banged out those words on the typewriter for the loose-leaf journal or diary of Bill's illness that I had begun to keep sporadically.

How did I know?

Because I had seen just as suddenly and just as clearly that the consultant had been wrong about another point. Maybe my subconscious had worked it out during the night, but at any rate I reasoned: If he can be wrong about one point, he can be wrong about two.

What was the other point?

My diary went on to explain that: "He said no messages get from the stem of Bill's brain to the motor-center. All wrong! During the last week or ten days Bill has moved his right leg, not just involuntarily, but when the nurses asked him to. And the other day I said to him, 'Now let's say morning prayers. Make the sign of the cross.' Without help from me he moved his right hand toward his forehead and then attempted to go from shoulder to shoulder.

"A couple of times too, he has taken my hand in his right hand and lifted it to his lips. His mind directs these motions. Why was I so flustered that I forgot to present this evidence to the consultant?"

Later, I did present the evidence to the Director, and he admitted that maybe "some" messages did get through because "some undamaged 'wires' still go from the brain stem to the motor-center," but he added, "That doesn't alter the fact that many other 'wires' have been destroyed, and no therapy can revitalize them."

I started to say that I thought enough "wires" were working to warrant strenuous therapy when the Director said very positively, "The best hope of Mr. Coakley's recovering any further function is bed rest and care."

Again I wrote in my diary, "O God! I feel so confused and muddleheaded with this contradictory advice that I can't decide St. Thomas or no. Well, I'll wait until the twenty-fifth and meanwhile keep praying."

On March twenty-fourth, lightning from heaven! When I went to Green Valley that morning, Marcella, one of the private-duty nurses announced, "Bill has SPOKEN! He said 'Hi' to a therapist."

Surely— oh surely, this was a signal— a shout from the Blessed Mother, saying to me: Keep working and hoping. Surely, she wouldn't have arranged for Bill to speak for the first time since he allegedly spoke in Balfour Hospital months before unless she were pointing toward St. Thomas.

No encore that day. But the next morning, the feast of the Annunciation when I went to Green Valley, Marcella told me that Bill had spoken two more words. She had asked him the color of his hospital gown and he had answered, "Yellow"; the color of her hair and he had answered, "Brown."

I myself had heard nothing whatever, but I had no hesitation about making a decision— or rather I felt the decision had been made for me: Go to St. Thomas Hospital.

Now the arrangements. As Step #1, I had to get a doctor on the St. Thomas staff to treat Bill and to admit him to that hospital. I told the Director my plans, and he offered to phone whichever St. Thomas doctor I wanted and make an appointment for the man to come to Green Valley to see Bill. I also talked to the St. Thomas doctor myself, and in just a couple of hours everything seemed to be set. Mission accomplished!

Nothing is ever that easy. Later in the day the St. Thomas doctor phoned me back and said, "The Director tells me that five doctors have declared your husband incapable of more therapy. There's no use in making the St. Thomas move. Why change beds? He wouldn't be able to cooperate with a therapist."

"But the Balfour Hospital doctors haven't seen my husband for months, and the picture has changed," I protested.

"The psychiatrist at Green Valley and the hospital Director have both told me that Mr. Coakley cannot cooperate with a therapist."

We batted the issue back and forth for at least five minutes; then the St. Thomas doctor said flatly, "I refuse to admit Mr. Coakley to my service."

Rightly or wrongly, I felt at this point that the Director was villain of the scene because obviously he had made a second call to the St. Thomas doctor and given him a negative picture of Bill. The next day I asked the Director if he would release Bill to St. Thomas if I managed to get another doctor on its staff to treat Bill.

"Certainly," he answered, "you have the prerogative to do that, but I think it's wasted effort and worse." He went on the umpteenth time with the "reality" lecture. I didn't bother to listen. I could have given the lecture myself, word for word.

More phone calls, and doctor-friends recommended another St. Thomas staff doctor. Bea C. said, "Let's go slowly and cautiously this time. I expect to see him in a couple of days. I'll give him the whole case history and tell him about Bill's recent astonishing progress. Then I'm sure I'll have no trouble making an appointment for you."

If that evening I went home feeling a trifle relieved, the next day I had reason to feel like dancing on the rooftop. I myself heard Bill speak! Just as casually as though he had been saying it every day for months, he greeted me in the morning with "Hi darl."

From then on I heard him speak every day. His words were

sparse — one or two in twenty-four hours — but I gloated over them as a miser gloats over gold.

Then there came further cause for joy. To my utter amazement the Director asked me, "Have I your permission to have the psychiatrist reevaluate Mr.Coakley for therapy?"

My permission! Good heaven, YES! Why not, if possible, get therapy for Bill while we were awaiting the St.Thomas move?

But what had caused this abrupt about-face? The speaking? I was too happy to ask.

The psychiatrist decided, "Mr.Coakley can take more therapy, and there's hope that he'll improve. The next two or three months will be crucial. I suggest too that the speech therapist reevaluate him."

Now I was absolutely sure of what I had been half-sure before: God was answering my prayers — not by an instant cure, but by installments. Well, whichever way He did it was fine with me. I could wait for the glorious end-result.

I phoned Cardelli to give him the latest news bulletins, including of course Bea's plan to make an appointment with the second St.Thomas doctor.

All systems were go — or so it seemed briefly. But somehow the old see-saw pattern could not be broken. The nurses noticed that Bill had begun to wince as though in pain every time they so much as touched his left arm. The Director ordered X-rays to see what was wrong.

The pictures showed no broken bones and no bursitis, and a cardiogram showed no heart disorder that could be the culprit. The Director told the nurses to put hot packs on the arm, and that helped slightly. Later, he brought in two others doctors to have a look.

The three men stood at the bedside stroking their chins or tugging at their ears and then concluded that a ligament had been torn, possibily by orderlies lifting Bill out of bed. It had not healed because of the weight of the paralyzed arm. They ordered a sling to keep the arm from pulling on the shoulder.

Two days of that, and Virginia, one of the private-duty nurses, said, "The arm is stiffer than ever."

Alarmed, I asked the Director to call in an orthopedist.

Naturally, I had shelved plans for the St. Thomas move, and I had told Bea to cancel the doctor's appointment. While Bill was in pain, it would be both absurd and cruel to consider "walking" therapy à la Cardelli.

When the orthopedist arrived, he said the shoulder had atrophied after the months of inactivity so that now, to move it even slightly, caused severe pain. "But," he said, "pain or no, we have to loosen it up with more, not less, passive-motion exercises. I'll prescribe sedation for the pain."

"How long will it take to loosen it up?" I asked, inwardly sighing about an indefinite delay of the move to St. Thomas.

"I can't say," came the expected answer.

So life continued a suspense story with St. Thomas Hospital, like the far horizon, receding with every step I walked toward it. I found out what Lacordaire[2] meant when he said, "Prayer keeps us from going mad." My sanity seemed to depend on the morning Mass on my way to Green Valley. Each day it seemed that some verse from the liturgy sustained me. One Sunday I noted in my journal that the Mass included, "They brought forth the sick into the streets, and laid them on beds and couches, that when Peter came, his shadow at the least might overshadow any of them, and they might be delivered from their infirmities."[3]

I thought: Peter is a great saint, "the Prince of the Apostles," but he's still on a lower rung than Mary is. God chose her of all creatures to bear in her body the body of the Lord; He chose her of all creatures to live under the same roof as Jesus for the thirty years of His hidden life. If St. Peter's mere shadow could call forth the power of God, surely I can count on Mary's intercession.

While I waited for the St. Thomas move and for the shoulder healing, I realized once again how much there was to pray for in Bill's case. I had the impression he saw me better when I stood on his right side. I mentioned this to nurse Virginia and she replied, "Yes, I've noticed that too." Then she hinted that the stroke might have left Bill blind in one eye.

Although the loss of one eye is not tragedy in itself, another handicap atop the rest did seem tragedy. Especially, I thought, it was tragedy for Bill. I didn't know for sure, but I doubted if people with only one sound eye would be able to read for long stretches of time. If Bill ever returned to anything like normal, limited reading would be to him a greater hardship than fifty-pound leg-irons would be to most people. In the past, I would fuss because he often read after we had gone to bed. Sometimes I'd put on an eye-shade and go to sleep, but sometimes I'd say, "For heaven's sake, aren't you ever going to turn off the light. You need your sleep; 6:30 comes mighty soon."

Whether he sighed resignedly and did as I asked, or whether he made some facetious remark and went on reading a while, he definitely believed no day, however full and busy, was complete without a ration of reading. That meant, if we went to a party or a show, and he hadn't touched a book all evening, he was the more likely to read in bed.

Thinking about all this, one day at Green Valley I almost dared to test Bill's eyes by holding my hand over his right eye and asking him if he could see with the left. But I couldn't do it. If he were blind in one eye, he'd be happier not knowing. I went home feeling unusually depressed that evening.

In the wee hours of the night, unable to sleep, I snapped on the bedside lamp and picked up a spiritual book that I had put on the night table a week before but hadn't so far dipped into. Now I opened it and my eyes lit upon the words of St. Francis de Sales, "Do not look forward to what might happen tomorrow ... The same everlasting Father ... Who cares for you today ... will take care of you tomorrow and every day. Either He will shield you from suffering, or He will give you unfailing strength to bear it. Be at peace then and put aside all anxious thoughts and imaginations."

It seemed to me that Christ was speaking to me. And every time I had been extra-low, it was as though He did the same thing. He didn't take away my troubles, but He gave me some thoughts, some words, that lightened them enough for me to go on. Prayer, I discovered, is not a monologue; when you speak to

Him, He speaks to you either through the thoughts He puts into your mind, or through the words of spiritual or scriptural writers. Sometimes, then, my part was to listen.

This wasn't a new idea to me. On my way to Green Valley Hospital I would often stop at a church, not only for Mass but just to sit there a few minutes without prayerful words, just gazing at the tabernacle hoping for the Voice. The Lord said, "Seek and you shall find."[4] What I found (not always instantly, but always eventually) was some answers, some relief, and some new strength.

That's what this book is all about. I want to say in its pages that God helps and sustains and guides you or, let me put the thought in the words of a poet, "The dark itself is starry with His grace."

So that night after reading St.Francis' words, I told myself: I must put Bill in the hands of his everlasting Father and mine. His future depends on God, not on me, nor on anything I can do.

This was, in effect, Bill's old Declaration of Dependence again. Though I tried to make the declaration that night as I had tried before, I knew that it was not something I could do and have it stay done. As sure as sunrise, my own ego would reassert itself, and I'd have to redo the whole job. As one sage person said, "The spiritual life is a series of beginnings."

{6}

The period of waiting for the shoulder pain to go away stretched through April and most of May, but it wasn't a flat, dull period. First of all, there were the "highs" whenever Bill spoke. Often in the beginning he spoke just one word at a time. He didn't mumble; he spoke distinctly, but Bill of the pre-stroke booming voice now spoke so softly we had to strain to catch what he was saying.

I was so afraid I'd miss one precious word that I decided to take a course in lipreading. Happily, that was much ado about nothing. I never had to take the course because just a few days after I made arrangements to sign up, Bill was speaking with more strength and was easily audible.

Then came the glorious day calling for a *Te Deum* when Bill began to use whole sentences. To me it was, "I love you." To nurse Marcella it was the answer, "No thank you."

At Mass the next day the Gospel was about Jesus walking on the water and about His chiding the apostles for lack of faith. I told myself I should have had more faith about Bill's talking again. It seemed to me now, if not to everybody else, that the installment plan miracle was indeed under way. The next event seemed to be another installment. The Director told me he was going to attempt removal of the gastro-nasal tube and then try feeding Bill orally.

Attempts had been made twice before, and each time Bill had nearly died. After the first attempt in Balfour in January, Bill had aspirated some orally-fed food and ended up with one of his "severe respiratory infections" which, to the "amazement" (their word) of the doctors, Bill survived. After the second attempt at Green Valley in February, he had again aspirated food, and the doctors proposed a gastrostomy (the surgical procedure of making an opening through the abdominal wall into the stomach to allow the introduction of nourishment). One afternoon the doctors asked my permission to perform the operation and gave me until morning to decide. But by morning surgery was out of the question. Because of food aspirated, Bill had developed bilateral pneumonia during the night and seemed to have only hours to live. Again, he "amazed" everybody and survived.

Terrified though I was of a third attempt to remove the tube, I knew that it had to be made sooner or later because several doctors had warned me the tube could cause dire throat troubles if it were to stay in indefinitely.

Removal day was May third. That morning at Mass when I said, "Give us this day our daily bread," I meant literally: Give Bill his daily *bread*, not liquid through a tube.

The attempt succeeded. That afternoon Bill had his first successful oral feeding since November.

For a change, I cried, not with sadness, but with joy. And it must have been an immense relief to Bill to be rid of that apparatus because as soon as the doctor had done his work, Bill said, "Thank you," and again "thank you, thank you."

That was a *long* speech for him, and it was obviously heart felt. But long speeches from then on became more and more usual. I counted the words, seven, twelve, fifteen, twenty-seven words a day; then happily I lost count. When my pastor paid a visit at this time, I had a silly, superstitious fear (of which I'm now a bit ashamed) of saying how much Bill was speaking as though my testimony would break a charm and put a jinx on progress.

There came a day soon after when we had our first tiny conversation. Now that Bill was eating, I had brought in oranges to squeeze some fresh juice which he used to like. As I was cutting the fruit in half, Bill said, "Be careful, honey. Don't cut yourself."

I replied in a light facetious tone, "Oh, you still love me."

He answered, "Damn right I do."

These bright moments lulled me into semiforgetfulness of brain damage. Besides, Bill's short three-or-four-word sentences had showed no brain damage. On the contrary, they had showed intelligence.

Soon *after* Bill began to speak, the speech-therapist stopped by Bill's room. He asked me about Bill's interests, and I mentioned that he had belonged to a group of men who met to read Shakespeare. The therapist turned to Bill and said, "'All the world's a ...' What comes next?"

"Stage," answered Bill.

I wanted to shout: Bravo!

Then the therapist asked some simple "two-plus-two-equals-what?" math problems. Bill answered several correctly before he stopped speaking either because he was tired or bored.

Finally, the therapist gave Bill a slate and asked him to write his name. Without hesitation Bill wrote, "Wm.D.Coakley."

"Try writing your wife's name," said the therapist.

I expected him to write "Mary," but I wouldn't have been surprised if he had written one of his many nicknames for me— "Angel-face," "Princess," "Lamb chop," "My favorite wife," or "My child-bride." Instead, he wrote formally, "Mary Lewis Coakley." The writing was legible, though it ran irregularly up hill and down dale.

But what impressed the speech-therapist was Bill's facility with words. "Many stroke patients have a hard time finding correct words to express their thought," he said. "Your husband comes out easily with the proper word, be it multisyllabled or unusual."

That was true. One day, asking the nurse to change his position (he still couldn't turn over in bed, nor sit up) he explained, "There's pressure on my coccyx bone."

But as he began to speak more at length, I should have realized that he was sometimes confused. In those early days of speech, I found a way to rationalize about anything that didn't make sense. The first time I felt real fear was the day he asked me to hand him his shoes because, he said, "I'm going to walk down the hall." Then I couldn't squelch the panicky thought: Isn't his mind clear enough to know that he can't even sit up, much less walk?

Yet even nurse Virginia argued against my fear. She said, "Before the shoulder kicked up, we nurses put his shoes on when he went to P.T. As for using the word 'walk,' that's natural, too. We lifted the foot-rest of his wheelchair and tried to get him to move his good right foot. Then as we rolled him down the hall we'd say 'Look, you're walking.'" She ended by saying, "I'm sure his mind is OK. All his comments show a high degree of intelligence."

Because I wanted to, I suppose, I believed her; the alternative was so dreadful. If his mind were badly impaired, and if the shoulder pain kept delaying his getting to St. Thomas Hospital and to the hope of walking again, the future was too black to contemplate.

The next morning, saying the joyful "Mysteries" of the rosary, I came to "The Presentation of the Infant Jesus in the Temple." In the prestroke past I had always meditated on the act of surrender to God, the Father, that Mary made in presenting her Son to Him, and I told myself that I must try to put my own life and will in God's hands. It was easy to do when things were going my way. Since the stroke, it was hard. Did God will that Bill be in a state of mental confusion? Did He will Bill to wait weeks before he had the benefit of Mr. Cardelli's therapy?

Still another morning I went to Mass with the same thoughts, but I realized then that whether I liked it or not, Bill's life and my life were in God's hands. We were finite creatures; He is omnipotent. True, He had given us a free will. I could rebel and say, "I know best," or I could say, "God, You know best." I wasn't changing things by the first statement; I was just showing a lack of trust in His goodness and His wisdom.

So I wrote in my diary, "If He allows Bill and me to suffer, He will compensate us a hundredfold some day— even it if is in another world. And perhaps if I could just make the surrender generously, He might cut short Bill's suffering and mine— for my good behavior as it were. Recently, I jotted down this quotation from the fourteenth century German spiritual writer, John Tauler, 'Give yourself wholly to God and He will give Himself wholly to you; renounce your will for His and He will do so for you. In everything abandon yourself to God and He will provide for all your needs and fulfill all your spiritual desires with a generosity and munificence beyond all human conception.'[1]

"Still I don't think I can quite do that. I keep envisioning the miracle, and May thirteenth, a feast of Our Lady of Fatima, that Therese speaks of, is almost here."

"Today the Mass prayers (which often give me a 'theme song' for the day) contained the verse, 'I will extol thee, O God my king: and I will bless thy name . . .'[1] It strikes me that I must be steadfast in praising and thanking Him all the days of my life if Bill is cured. In fact, I should say more prayers of thanks right now, for there is no *earthly* reason that the doctors can see for Bill to have spoken. Actually, in right-handed people, the left hemisphere of the brain (which in Bill's case is the more damaged hemisphere) controls speech.

"But I'm strongest, not on praise and thanks, but on the perennial cry 'Help!' Well, maybe a few 'Helps' aren't bad either. Thomas Merton in his book, *The Seven Storey Mountain*, calls it a form of pride never to petition for our needs. It is, he said, a 'subtle way of trying to put ourselves on the same plane as God — acting as though we had no needs, as if we were not creatures, not dependent on Him . . .'"[2]

The Lord must have heard at least some of my cries. Bill began for the first time to move his weak left leg ever so slightly.

As for as his mental confusion — well, I still wasn't sure (the wish being father to the thought) that it was really confusion. I don't remember how long I went on finding some means of explaining it away. Anyhow, I know I was still doing it some days later when I brought a portable TV to the hospital. I then said to a friend who had dropped into see Bill, "I haven't put this on yet. I don't know whether Bill would enjoy it."

In a split second, before the friend had a chance to say anything, Bill spoke up, "If there's a football game on, I'd enjoy it."

The friend said, "Bill, there isn't any football now," where-upon Bill said, "There should be. It's football season."

Though at first I thought sadly: He doesn't realize it's spring; he's confused, I soon rationalized that it was November when he had the CVA. Having been comatose over five months, he couldn't be aware of the passage of time. It's logical for him to suppose it's football season.

But in due course the fact was forced upon me that he had no sense of time whatever and that he never knew whether it was morning or afternoon, much less fall or spring. Then, despite the fact that he remembered much of the distant past, he had almost no ability to record recent events. When friends came to see him, he forgot that they had been there as soon as the door closed behind them.

Worst of all, in my opinion, he never asked me what was wrong with him, or why he was in the hospital, or which hospital he was in, or anything about his condition. Once or twice he mentioned having broken his leg and his hip, and I couldn't bear to say, "No, you haven't broken any bones. You had a cere-bral hemorrhage." I let that go for a few more months.

Meantime, I could not deny that there were other little men-tal aberrations. Each one brought a stab of pain to me.

One evening as I was leaving for home, he said, "Wait a min-ute honey. I'll go with you and drive you there."

A lump came into my throat, but I managed to mumble that I'd changed my mind and wasn't going home just then after all. Then I began to talk about something else. I had noticed that he was easily distractible and apparently couldn't hold one thought long.

Another time when I came in, in the morning, he said, "Oh, I'm so glad to see you! I didn't think you'd come because I didn't think you knew where I was."

Still another time he declared, "Bob came to see me. He left some cookies in the garage."

Bob, a good friend, had indeed been by, but he had left no cookies, and the "garage" Bill must have had in mind was our own at home, six or seven miles away.

The next day, he said, "Did you bring my clothes? I'm going home tomorrow."

When I didn't answer instantly, he went on, "Where will you be tomorrow? I'm going down town. I have to go to the office as usual."

Then one afternoon when I announced that a couple we knew were coming to see him, he answered, "Isn't it time for me to get up and get dressed? We're going out to dinner with them, aren't we?"

Marcella, who usually wasn't optimistic, thought these mental flights were temporary, and she kept commenting on the many times he was "extraordinarily sharp." Virginia, on the other hand, although she had been very optimistic in the beginning, thought them permanent. Two nurses who substituted over weekends agreed with Virginia.

Incidentally, he was worse one Saturday in early May than he had been at any time before. At one point he got the identities of Joe, our grandson Billy, and his brother mixed up. I was so upset that I had to leave the room and step into the hall. One of the nurses found me sobbing there and said, "What else can you expect of a man who has had a cerebral hemorrhage?"

Her words didn't help any, but I was helped a little later when (after I'd returned to Bill's room) he seemed to pull himself back to reality by saying, "I'm confused."

At least he knew he had gotten off the track.

That evening I had a long distance call from a friend whose husband had had a stroke some years before and had lived perhaps five years afterwards. I told her, "Bill's mind is like a TV screen. Sometimes it shows a clear sharp picture, other times a blurred one, or the picture fades or jumps erratically."

She answered, "I know just what you mean. Though Fred wasn't as bad physically as Bill is, he had confused moments until the day he died."

That didn't lift my spirits. I went to bed in tears.

I never asked the Director the "permanent or temporary" question. I figured he wouldn't know the answer. I had been reading some books on the brain that supported Cardelli's opinion that the brain is too complex for any doctor to be able, at this stage of medical knowledge, to give many positive opinions. One writer had said that no scientist or group of scientists could "understand the whole cortex, and it may take years to explore an area no bigger than a postage stamp." This writer spoke too of the brain containing thirteen billion cells which is "five times more than the number of people in the world." And another writer spoke of "a hundred billion glia or neurological cells in the cerebrum and about ten billion nerve cells." Still another wrote that if all the brain's nerve cells and fibers were strung end to end they would reach to the moon and back."

I would just wait and see — and meantime pray. Always it came back to that.

Finally dawned the thirteenth— Miracle Day?

Driving to Green Valley I half-chanted one of my standbys, "I do believe, Lord, help my unbelief."[1]

Once at the hospital I could see no change in Bill, but the whole day lay ahead. I watched and waited with high spirits. Even after I got home that evening at the end of an uneventful day, my spirits were still fairly buoyant. Joe and Jeanne phoned, and Jeanne spoke the very words that were in my mind, "The day isn't really over until midnight."

When we hung up though, I began to feel less confident of a miracle, and by the time I was ready to go to bed a couple of hours later, I was pretty low. Still I told myself: I may yearn for an instant cure, but who am I to dictate to God? He seems to be granting at least an installment plan cure. How long will that take? And when will the final installment come— if ever? Therese, when she first mentioned focusing on the thirteenth, added, "God's timing may not synchronize with ours, but it is His timing that is always perfect."

Then came another thought: Something could have happened after I left Green Valley, and nobody has told me yet. The private-duty nurse leaves at eleven, and then until the other P.D. nurse comes at seven in the morning, floor-nurses tend Bill. Since they're less closely connected with the case, they might not phone me, or maybe since they pop into his room only at intervals and stay very briefly, they may not notice any marked change.

But the next morning when I went to Green Valley, I could see for myself there was no change. I tried to fight back tears. I felt as though prayer were useless, a waste of time, and indeed I might have stopped praying, if I hadn't felt as Peter did when he said, "to whom shall we go?"[2] I had no one but Him.

Was there something wrong with the way I prayed? I was praying earnestly, eagerly, avidly for a cure, but I asked myself: How much love of God is in my prayer? Faith, yes. Hope, yes. But love? There is love for Bill and love for myself, but love of God isn't conspicuous. I'm concentrating so intently on my longing for the gift of a cure that I'm in danger of overlooking the Great Giver, God, and His longing to give the best to Bill and me. If I truly loved God, I'd end all prayers with Jesus' words, "not as I will, but as thou *wilt.*"[3] That was *so* hard for me to say.

During the next days at least I clung to my habit of culling other scriptural words from the Mass to say and to try to live by.

The Eucharist too sustained me more surely than any food I cooked on my own stove or selected in Green Valley cafeteria. I understood, as I never had before, the verse, "my flesh is meat indeed: and my blood is drink indeed."[4]

One day as I prayed after Communion, the second joyful "Mystery" of the rosary (the visit of the pregnant Blessed Mother Mary to her pregnant cousin Elizabeth) crossed my mind. Elizabeth "cried out with a loud voice . . . saying . . . the infant in my womb leaped for joy."[5] I thought: I've just received Jesus in my heart this minute. I'll go right to Green Valley and I'll take Jesus to Bill. (The church I attended was only a five-minute drive away.) If His presence made the unborn John leap in his mother's womb, surely it will affect Bill.

After that I rushed out of church each morning; I could hardly wait to reach Bill and kiss him. Yet day followed day and nothing spectacular happened; I saw only snail-like progress. Bill's shoulder was somewhat better, he was moving more in bed, and therapists were giving him more leg exercises. As for his erratic mental state, no change. Often after I got home at night, I'd type out an example or two of his uneven conversation to slip into the loose-leaf binder that served as my diary. One day I had Beethoven's Fifth Symphony on the radio I'd put in Bill's room. (Since the early comatose days of Balfour, I had played his beloved classical music in his room, hoping it would "do something" for him.) Bill remarked about "the English-horn solo." Then I gave an accolade to the violinists and he answered, "They're good, but I think the soloist is super." I asked then, as though I didn't know, "Who is your favorite composer?" and he said, "This stuff is hard to beat. Beethoven comes close to the top. I like the other Bs' too, Bach and Brahms. Wagner comes rather far down on my list."

This sounded like the prestroke Bill! Yet when I was leaving a few hours later, he said to me, "I'll meet you at home."

A friend advised, "Thank God for whatever happens, even Bill's momentary confusion, because He has some good purpose in allowing it."

To thank God for this seesaw seemed beyond me, but from the beginning I had admitted to myself that the illness might be a spiritual boon to Bill. A few weeks before the stroke he and I were discussing world affairs, and he said, "Man has gotten himself into such a mess that it seems only God can pull him out."

"You're saying what the Blessed Mother said at Fatima," I answered. "Her formula for world peace and order was: Pray and do penance. Maybe you and I should pray more."

"Umm . . ."

"Well, we could devote some time every Sunday afternoon to special prayers and meditation."

"I'm not very good at meditation. My mind jumps all over like fleas on a dog. But here's a counter suggestion. How about my reading aloud for twenty minutes or so from some spiritual book and then the two of us discussing it?"

We actually did do this a couple of times and the Sunday before the CVA Bill read from *My Way of Life*, which is Walter Farrell, O.P.'s condensation and simplification of Thomas Aquinas' *Summa*. Afterwards we were talking about accepting God's will. Bill said, "There's one thing we can do here and now. We can accept the time and the manner of our own death.

We can tell the Lord that His plan, whatever it is, is OK with us."

"Oh, for heaven's sake!" I exclaimed. "How morbid can you get?" (I had been thinking about accepting the nasty rainy weather.)

"When we do get sick," Bill said, "who knows how capable we'll be of conscious compliance?"

Remembering what he said, I had long believed that every moment he lay upon his hospital bed, he was in a sense offering himself up like a living sacrifice. He was suffering for Christ. Then, because he was suffering *for* Christ, he was suffering *with* Christ and his sufferings took on an enormous value and won for him innumerable graces. Christ said, "In my Father's house there are many mansions . . ."[6] and I believed that one of the best had Bill's name on the doorpost. Still I didn't want him to claim his inheritance just yet. I wanted him here with me in good health. And whether a person dies for Christ or lives for Christ, in either case he gives his life for Christ. In sum, that's what it means to be a Christian, or a Christ-follower.

Yes, I desperately wanted and prayed for Bill to live and to recover. But there was so much to recover, including that item still high on my worry list, his sight. One afternoon, I read him a newspaper clipping. Then I laid the clipping on the arm of my chair by the bed. Bill reached for the scrap of paper saying, "I'll read it myself."

I made a dive for it, too, and somehow managed to get there ahead of him, saying, "Oh, the light in here is bad, and you're sick. Let me read it to you again."

The incident left me trembling. Although it was a step toward normalcy for him to want to read himself, I was terrified that he would find out he couldn't. That night I remembered the blind man in the gospels who begged, "Rabboni, that I may see,"[7] and I begged, "Lord, that Bill may see."

The Lord did send something heartening the next day. On May twentieth (I wrote the date in my diary) when I arrived at the hospital, I announced to Bill, "Ogden Nash died."

Instantly, Bill answered, "He's the one who said, 'Candy is dandy, but liquor is quicker.'"

"Yes," I took up eagerly, "and he's the one who said, 'Parsley is gharsley.'"

Since Bill didn't immediately respond to that, I prodded, "There were verses you used to recite about riches, about writers, about . . ."

Bill began:

> When I was young, (or maybe five)
> And glad, so glad to be alive
> Oh, how my fancy used to itch
> To be— how shall I say it?— rich![8]

He broke off and said, "But Ogden Nash didn't write that!"

I looked it up when I got home, and Bill had been right. Samuel Hoffenstein had written the verse about riches.

Definitely, here was the old Bill! All those rhymes, limericks, ditties, anecdotes, as well as serious quotations that his blotter-like memory had once absorbed were apparently still intact. Why, he even remembered who wrote what! Now at last he was out of the fog. A wave of joy engulfed me, and I felt: This is one of the happiest days of my entire life.

Now, if Bill's mind were OK, I decided, he'd enjoy more intellectual stimulation. He had been a Civil War buff, and in his den he had several hundred volumes on the subject. The TV University of the Air program had a series of lectures at 6:30 A.M. about battles of the war, so I set my alarm clock and began to get up earlier than usual every morning to tune in and tape the lectures for replay to Bill later. Also, I got the Talking Books for the Blind, which are records of full-length books to be played on a phonograph.

How much Bill understood I'm not sure now. I learned all too soon that there had indeed been permanent brain damage. I could not play any fiction for Bill because by the time the record reached Chapter Two, Bill had forgotten Chapter One and didn't know who the characters in the story were. In short, like a senile person, he had no memory for the immediate past, but he could recall facts stored up years before. I chose, then, Talking Books which were duplicated in our own library and which I knew Bill had read. He could follow history books to a degree. He had almost no ability to learn new facts. Nor was he any longer the Bill with the quick, incisive judgment, the keen analytical mind, but, like the sun trying to break through dark clouds, he showed occasional glimpses of him. I lived for those glimpses.

I explained this to my sister Katharine and her husband, Paul, who came up to Pennsylvania in late May to visit me. Of course, Bill knew them, but when they told him that *en route* they had stopped in Nashville to see our son Joe, Bill said to me, "Don't you think it's odd that Joe's in town, and I haven't seen him?"

I tried to tell him that Joe was still in Tennessee, but Bill remained hurt that Joe hadn't been to see him. I said "remained hurt," but actually Bill didn't keep any thought for long.

While Katharine and Paul were in town I talked to the head-therapist at Green Valley one day, and he used the now-hackneyed word "amazed." He said, "We're all amazed around here that Mr. Coakley has come as far as he has. I can't say if he will continue to improve, but let's hope."

Hope! Yes, I kept hoping at least for the installment-plan miracle, although at times I thought I was kidding myself. Certainly, Katharine and Paul thought I was kidding myself. Paul remarked that expecting a cure was like expecting a ninety year old arthritic to be as spry as a twenty year old athlete. There had been irreversible physical changes.

Katharine said, "You discount so much that the doctors say," and I had to nod in agreement. What she said was perfectly true. I figured doctors knew the hard, cold facts about disease they had learned in med school. They knew too, through experience, how *most* patients react to disease, but they didn't know Bill and his spirit and his determination, and more important they didn't take into account the possibility of supernatural intervention. Or maybe I should say that I believed doctors absolutely and implicitly when they said *they* couldn't do anything for Bill, and that was the reason I needed a miracle. It was the only possiblity left. My theory has always been: Do what you can; and what you can't do, leave to God. Then, there was a third thing that made me less than attentive to doctors. Half the time I knew I couldn't understand what they were saying. My emotions paralyzed my mind and then there was no absorbing medical explanations though they were made in words of one syllable.

But Katharine and Paul were less concerned about my accepting reality than about the financial strain I was under and would be under to a greater degree when the insurance money ran out. To cut expenses they suggested, "Sell the house and find an apartment nearby where you can live on less." And they urged speed, explaining, "When the hot weather comes, people don't go house-hunting. June is a better month to sell than July."

At the same time, they kept urging me, "Take care of yourself."

To my mind, their advice seemed contradictory. A move would mean cleaning out closets, cellar, and attic and sorting over everything I owned, the accumulation of thirty-some years of marriage, deciding: Keep this, sell this, give this away, or throw this away. That would require endless hours of work, so it would be harder than ever to take care of myself. Moreover, selling the house would be tearing to shreds visible reminders of life-with-Bill. The place held so many happy memories of our "togetherness." Lastly I thought: If the day comes, as I hope it will eventually, when I bring Bill home, it will be easier to manage in a house than in a tiny, cramped apartment where the nurses and I would probably bump into one another with every step. Then too, I'd never have a moment's privacy— privacy to cry, to think, to pray, or to write in my journal.

The last wasn't insignificant. Writing helped me to take the dark wad of pain from my heart and lay it before me on the table where I could sort out the confused thoughts that wound around it. I empathized totally with Anne Morrow Lindbergh who said (in *Locked Rooms and Open Doors*) "The habit of writing . . . in my diary . . . probably saved my sanity . . . I must write it *out* at any cost." (Emphasis added).

As for curtailing my visits to the hospital, which Katharine and Paul proposed as a take-care-of-yourself measure, that was impossible; I couldn't do it. Being with Bill was my daily sustenance. True, I hated spending hours and hours in the (to me) depressing place of tears, heartbreak, and suffering (I even hated its odor, compounded of disinfectant, ether, floor wax, soap, urine, and heaven knows what else), and I came home every evening emotionally and physically drained. However, when I was at home in the empty house, I could hardly contain myself until it was time to go back to Bill.

Katharine and Paul were so prodigiously kind, generous, and compassionate that I felt I should heed their advice about selling the house. Reluctantly then, before they left town, I put the house on the market.

Immediately, I faced another decision: was it time to adopt the St. Thomas-Cardelli plan? There was no doubt that I still wanted Mr. Cardelli to work with Bill some way, some time, but . . . *now*? Bill's shoulder was far better, and I thought he could take more therapy than he was getting at Green Valley. And yet I was torn in two directions over this decision, too. I could not quite ignore the Director's opinion. The drip, drip, drip of his words had bored an entrance into my mind. He had told me many times in the past, and he was still telling me that I should allow Bill to gain strength by rest before I thought of strenuous therapy, and he hinted something dreadful might happen if I didn't. On the other hand, Mr. Cardelli, whom instinctively I trusted, seemed to imply: The sooner, the better.

As I hesitated, I saw more clearly than before that therapy, even of the Cardelli variety, whenever it came, would be a long drawn-out ordeal, so I asked Mr. Cardelli, "What if I put Bill in St. Thomas now, and then a few weeks from now that hospital, like any other regular hospital, refuses to keep him longer? What then? I'd have to bring him back to Green Valley, or find a regular nursing home. In neither case could I get him to you for therapy."

"You could put him into The Hill House Nursing Home," he answered. "I supervise therapy there. I go there at least twice a week."

I didn't like that scenario either. Bill wasn't a pawn to be moved from place to place. Besides if the Director *were* right about Bill's gaining strength with rest at Green Valley, then when I finally got him to St. Thomas, Cardelli's work would go faster, Bill could skip Hill House, and be able to come home directly from the St. Thomas hospitalization. If and when Bill came home, Cardelli had said that, although he couldn't come to the house often himself, he would send his aides several times a week, and he would supervise their work every step of the way.

While I was living in this twilight zone of indecision and fear of failing to choose the proper fork of the road, I talked to the physiatrist and he said, "I think there's been some slight improvement even within the last few days. When orderlies transfer Mr. Coakley from bed to wheelchair, he definitely tries to help himself."

"Do you think he will ever learn to walk?" I asked.

"We may know more in a month or two," he answered. "The nurses say you pray for your husband. Well, whatever you do, keep it up. It seems to be working."

A day or so later, the Lord sent at least a mini-miracle-installment; nurse Virginia managed, without the help of an orderly, to get Bill from bed to wheelchair. She said, "I told Mr. Coakley, 'You've got to help me,' and apparently he's capable of some small effort. It makes all the difference."

Soon she tried again, and she said, "When he cooperates, I can do it. When he doesn't, I can't, and I doubt if any one person could."

Nurse Geraldine (Gerry)— although she, until now, nursed Bill only as a substitute for the regulars, Marcella, Virginia, and Anna— tried too. Again success!

Marcella had a go at it and she, like the others, succeeded.

Suddenly, I knew just what I had to do. Like the face hidden in the puzzle, I found the answer or the decision staring up at me. I should by-pass *both* St. Thomas and The Hill House and bring Bill straight home. Then Cardelli could make house calls.

I began to talk to everybody who had nursed Bill to find out who was willing to try the bed-wheelchair transfer and who was willing to do home nursing. Because nobody can be expected to work seven days a week, thirty-one days a month, there had to be substitutes along with the two regulars. Marcella, Virginia, Gerry and a male nurse named Hugh (whom Bill called "Pat" because of his Irish brogue) took my job offer.

I was rather sorry I had put the house on the market. Happily I had asked top dollar for it. Within a week I had had a bid that was a few thousand below my price. I turned it down. The would-be buyer then raised the bid, and again I turned it down.

Joe said, "Mother, that's not the way you do it. You negotiate. The bidder names a price, and you name a price higher than his, but less than your original asking price. If you want to sell, you handle it like a horse trade."

At his words I realized that I didn't want to sell. As soon as I hung up the phone after my conversation with Joe, I dialed the real estate agent and asked how soon I could take my house off the market.

Then I shifted into high gear. I phoned Cardelli and confirmed the fact that he would give Bill therapy at home. He said, "I'll come with my aides, and I'll probably be there five minutes after the ambulance drives in the driveway."

I talked to the orthopedist once more, and he said there was no danger of the shoulder atrophying again as long as the nurses and I kept up the passive arm exercises.

Since I was taking Bill home, I didn't have to bother getting a doctor on St. Thomas staff to care for him, *but* I did have to find a doctor who would make house calls and who would OK therapy. I phoned a doctor-friend, Jack, and he willingly said, "Yes," on both counts. (Incidentally, our good friend, Alberta, had told me that Jack had said, "In my forty years of practice

I've never seen a case as severe as Bill's where the patient lived and made such progress." That made me feel Jack would be optimistic about further progress.)

I ordered a hospital bed, a wheelchair, and other sickroom gear from a medical-supply store.

I got in touch with a friend who has several stalwart sons and asked the boys to shift furniture and clear a bedroom for the equipment I'd ordered.

Of course I also found time to tell the Director my plans, and to order the ambulance to take Bill home.

On homecoming-day-minus-one I skipped Mass; I had to stay at home to accept delivery of the sickroom equipment. While I was waiting, I took out my old Missal and read the Mass prayers of the day, June fifteenth. The *Introit* was, "Many are the afflictions of the just; but out of them all will the Lord deliver them."[9] I felt that Bill was just, so the Lord was going to deliver him.

The next day, June sixteenth, when Bill actually did come home, I told Marcella, "I'm as excited as though I were getting married."

As I said the words, I realized that I loved Bill a thousand times more than on the day I did marry him. My love had grown, as I suppose does all true love, from day to day, from year to year, throughout marriage. I read once that "Love is what you've been through together." Though I might give a fuller definition, that one is great in so far as it goes.

On the big day itself, since there was ample time before the ambulance would pick up Bill, I went to Mass as usual. The first prayer to rivet my attention was, "The Lord became my protector . . . he brought me forth into a large place: he saved me, because he was well pleased with me."[10]

An omen? It must mean that bringing Bill home was going to set him free from his illness. Once again my spirits soared in hope.

Marcella rode in the ambulance with Bill while I went on ahead in my car so that I could have the house door open for the men to carry Bill in on a stretcher.

We had hardly gotten Bill inside and settled in bed when the doorbell rang. Good as his word, there was Mr.Cardelli with another therapist beside him.

Despite my visits to him at St.Thomas, and despite my many, many phone calls, he had never seen Bill. I wondered if he would find Bill's case tougher than he expected. I held my breath as he tested Bill's arms and legs. But afterwards he turned to me and said, "Mr.Coakley has some self-motion even in his weak left leg. He will walk."

That was the first time I had heard that categorical statement. I think I was too choked up to answer it.

Then Mr.Cardelli and his assistant got Bill out of bed and "walked" him some seven or eight steps across the room. I had never seen Bill "walked" more than two steps since the stroke. I knew then for sure, for sure, for sure, that Bill was now on his way.

The future seemed spangled with stars.

{8}

If anybody had asked me, "Are you glad to have Bill home?" I could have answered with the utmost sincerity, "Oh yes, yes, yes!"

Psychologically, there was far less strain now that we were together where we belonged. It was a blessed joy and relief to have him at my side.

Physically though, there was more strain. I found myself on a treadmill of cooking meals for nurses, pureeing food for Bill (his swallowing still wasn't perfect), running load after load of sheets, towels, pads, and so on through the clothes washer, dashing out to the grocery, and . . . and . . .

After strenuous days came "night-duty." I had nurses sixteen hours, between 7 A.M. and 11 P.M., and I acted as well as I could as night nurse. My job was to get up three times in my eight-hour "shift," change Bill's position in bed (since he still couldn't turn over) and, if necessary, replace wet pads with dry. At Green Valley I had fairly often helped a nurse move Bill so I knew the stress and effort of being a human derrick. Bill, a fairly big man, weighed 185 in prestroke days; I weighed 117 pounds. With a few tricks I'd learned from hospital personnel I could manage, so this wasn't so bad. Something else, however, was bad.

Though Bill was mostly rational during the day, at night, particularly in the beginning, he was more than confused; he was wildly irrational. Since the day of the CVA, I had rarely seen him beyond the witching hour, so I was unprepared for those first nights. He seemed to become a different person, a stranger, a crazed creature. I was both flabbergasted and frightened.

Between 2 A.M. and 4 A.M. of the first night home, he called me literally every minute or two, shouting, "Get rid of this fence. I won't be penned in."

He meant the rails of the hospital-type bed, similar to the rails he had had at Green Valley Hospital. There was no reasoning with him, and I was afraid to lower the rails. Although Bill was unable to turn, I couldn't take the chance of his somehow slipping off the bed and landing on the floor. I tried to soothe him and then go back to my own bed in an adjoining room, but as soon as I left him, he would call me again, and he would keep on calling me till I came, all the while shaking the rails with his good right hand and making a nerve-wracking din. I then decided to stay with him, but that didn't help. He kept repeating his demand about the rails and shaking them violently to punctuate every word he spoke. Sometimes, he would stop for two or three minutes, or even five minutes, and I would sigh with relief and say inwardly: Thank God! He has gone to sleep at last. But then as I made a stealthy move to go back to my bed, he would start up once more with the din.

The next day nurse Gerry and I dragged an extra mattress beside Bill's bed, figuring it might then be safe to lower the rails. The other side of the bed we could push up against the wall. I then expected better nights.

Instead the nights were worse. Bill developed a strange rash. It peppered his body, including his arm pits, his ears, his hands — everything.

It itched so badly that he constantly scratched himself with his good right hand. I feared infection. The first night after the rash appeared, I lay on his bed with him and tried to calm him and to hold his right hand. He was trembling all over, and it seemed as though he had one little spasm after another. Finally, he fell asleep and I crept back to my bed, too unnerved to settle down and sleep.

I called the doctor the next morning, and after he examined Bill, he said with refreshing candor, "Mary, I haven't the faintest idea what it is. But I'll give Bill some sedative pills that should keep him from scratching, and I'll prescribe a salve that I think may well be soothing."

We doled out the pills at intervals according to the directions and Bill, despite his slight swallowing difficulty managed to get them down.

The problem was that the effect of the first pill would wear off before the second pill was due. Then Bill, frenzied with the itching, often scratched himself until he bled.

Should we put gloves on him?

Nurse Virginia preferred to tie his right hand.

Then another miracle? In his frantic effort to scratch himself, Bill moved his left hand— not much, but some— the first time since the stroke.

It was something to cheer about, too, though it wasn't a miracle when we found a dermatologist willing to come to the house. He prescribed for Bill and the rash cleared up. Bill and I both had better nights.

No change in the days. I learned what a twenty-hour workday is like, seven days a week, thirty-one days a month, with no end in sight. I didn't take time and energy to write in my diary. My writing consisted mainly of writing checks for nurses and therapists and filling out forms for insurance claims.

Actually, it was nearly two months after Bill got home before I recorded anything in my diary, and then I listed laconically one day's schedule almost in the same way that the nurses kept a chart. Except for the fact that the day ended with my first outing in months, I said in the diary that it was a "typical day."

My account went like this:

Washed Bill's face; changed bedpads

Got B's breakfast

Gerry arrived 7 A.M.; ate my own breakfast; made my bed.

Put in load of wash.

Phoned Erma and arranged to go with her to Writers Guild meeting tonight.

Went out: P.O. to mail back talking books

Supermarket

Library to pick up book about handicapped man.

(Hope book has something in it that will help B.)

Home again. G. said broker phoned. Returned call and gave order to sell some stock.

G. & I put B. through passive range-of-motion exercises.

G. left. (To save money, I'm down to one shift of nursing a day, so she's splitting her shift and will return this evening so I can go out.)

Put clothes in dryer.

Got lunch. When I took it up to B., he had fallen asleep.

Ate my own lunch. Kept B.'s warm.

Started to make out checks to pay some bills.

B. woke up. Handed him urinal. He pushed it away with "No thanks, not now."

Soon wet himself.

Got him up. I've learned to make the transfer from bed to wheelchair.

Changed bed.

Gave him lunch.

Put sheets in washer. Put away clothes washed in morning.

Boy came to clip shrubbery and mow lawn. No plastic bag handy for clippings. Went to attic and dumped contents of a bag so I could give it to my young gardener.

By this time, it was 3:30. Therapist due at 4. Started to get things lined up for dinner so that when therapist left I could serve pronto. One pot on stove and it began to rain. Rushed out to get blanket on clothes line.

Therapist arrived. (Bill needs only one therapist now to walk him.) While he was here Marie and Eleanor dropped by. We had glass of sherry. M. and E. left.

Put things in dryer.

Finished getting dinner.

Therapist left and B. and I ate.

Gerry arrived as I was loading dish-washer.

Got things from dryer.

Dressed and went out.

Home at midnight.

Gerry had mislaid her car keys, so *long* search for them.

To bed shortly before 1 A.M. Felt I could outsleep Rip Van Winkle.

Around 3 B. called me for the first time of the night.

Now, I must say that I don't think I could have survived those hectic days without my wonderful friends, Ruth, Alberta, Florence, Marie, Barbara and *many, many, many others,* who kept up a steady stream of "care-packages" (as Joe called them)— a cake, some custard, a pot of stew, a casserole, all prepared. The kindness we received put me to shame because I had never been that solicitous about friends in trouble. One generous and imaginative friend, Josie, knowing how often I ran up and down stairs to get food and drink for Bill, sent me a small refrigerator that I could keep in his bedroom. Another friend, Betty, knowing I couldn't get out to buy clothes for myself, brought me some of her own ultra-chic dresses that she said she was tired of. They looked as though she had scarcely worn them.

Even though I received so much solicitude, Joe worried that I might get sick with my on-call-twenty-four-hours job. I realized then, as I never had before, that whenever you carry a load, God Himself lends a hand. You are not alone. Then too, as I told Joe, I was fired by a fierce incentive: I wanted to take care of Bill, and the strength of my desire gave strength to my body.

At the same time though, I took care of myself. I gulped vitamin pills conscientiously, and sometimes one of the nurses would give me an injection of B-12. Whenever I had a nurse on duty until 11 P.M., I had an early dinner, preceded by a stiff drink to make me drowsy, and went to bed at 7 P.M. Then when she was ready to leave she would open my bedroom door to signal me that I was now alone with Bill— "on night duty."

These days, and broken-sleep nights, are now partially a blur in my memory, and if I didn't have my journal's sporadic entries, I wouldn't be able to reconstruct the period at all.

After the maddening rash, which left as suddenly as it came, Bill cooperated well with the therapists, and he did even better when Mr. Cardelli himself showed up. Happily, the "Big Boss" didn't limit his visits to the "every couple of weeks," he had mentioned. He came at least once a week. As one of his aides said, "Mr. Cardelli simply can't keep away from the extra-tough cases. They're a challenge to him."

He used a top-sergeant approach. He swore at Bill and barked out orders, "Kick that leg. What's the matter with you? Can't you hear me? Are you lazy, or stupid, or what? Kick! I say kick! You do as I say. I give the orders, see? And I'm the best therapist in the world."

Once after a tirade of some length, he asked Bill, "Would you call me a bastard?"

Instantly and coolly Bill answered, "No, because I didn't know your parents."

As our friend Bea C. said, "Brain damage or no, Bill can still come out with answers that make you think: I wish I'd said that."

Seeing "Big Boss" pressure tactics, I agonized for Bill and often clenched my teeth so I wouldn't cry out: Stop it! Stop it! You're cruel. You're inhuman. You can't torture my husband any more.

I was able to keep mum only because I saw that this dynamic man, Cardelli, intensely wanted to help Bill, and he could not bear to see him put forth anything less than his absolute maximum effort. Bill didn't "kick" on command, but he soon did "move" his foot on his own, without anyone lifting it for him.

We were fortunate to have such a therapist — no not "fortunate," but "blessed." In prestroke days if I said, "We're fortunate," or "We're lucky," Bill would come back, "No, honey, we're blessed."

We were blessed, too, in the nurses. Each in her own individual and different way helped Bill. My journal records that one midsummer day, after Virginia got Bill to a sitting position on the side of the bed, she took her hand away. Though she stood ready to catch him if need be, Bill grabbed the head of the bed with his right hand and sat upright without any help. Another first!

I hope I said "*Deo gratias*," but maybe I didn't. I didn't do much vocal praying in those days. I hoped that my work offered to God served as prayer. After all, spiritual writers say prayer is not only talking to God; it is living in Christ. ("And I live, now not I; but Christ liveth in me . . . ."[1]); it is being imbued with His Holy Spirit and oriented toward the Godhead.

Of course I never got to weekday Mass, but once in a blue moon I did find time to read the Mass prayers from my old Missal. One day when I did, I noted in my diary the words, "The mercies of the Lord I will sing forever."[2]

Since Bill made headway steadily, there was something to sing about. (He even gained some bladder control.) His walking "amazed" everybody. He arrived at the point where he needed only one therapist to support him on the left side when he walked. I recorded some of Virginia's comments in my diary:

"The Green Valley doctors were right when they said whatever recovery there is usually comes during the first three to four months. I've done lots of nursing, and I've never seen this kind of recovery this late. Last April when we began the passive range-of-motion exercises I asked myself: Why are we bothering? This man will never get any better. In fact, most patients who've been in a coma as long as he was are a total mess.

"When people ask me if there can be any more improvement, I always say, 'Who knows? This is a special case. All rules are off.'"

Certainly, it was a special case. I figured the Blessed Mother's hand in it made it special, and she had enlisted some very special lieutenants, Mr. Cardelli and his team. These therapists worked with Bill until I was sure their backs must be ready to snap in two. One of the aides said, "Mr. Coakley's improvement bears out the boss' theory about strenuous walking therapy stimulating recovery on all fronts."

I expected further improvement. Marcella felt it wise to temper my optimism, and she said, "I think he's gotten as far as he can go. He has no sense of balance."

Well, he did list to the left — no doubt about that. But I asked a Cardelli aide what he thought. He answered, "Oh, Mr. Coakley will walk alone soon — using a cane, of course. The power is there."

Later, I told Bill, "I know the exact day, hour, and minute when you will walk. Do you know it?"

He shook his head no.

I answered, "The day, hour, and minute will be the very one when you say to yourself, 'I can and will walk.'"

Bill, like Cardelli, was the kind of person who rose to a challenge.

One day toward the end of July an aide was walking Bill; Bill was leaning heavily on his cane in his right hand, and the aide was giving him minimal support on the left side. Then the aide took away his hand and Bill walked on . . . a step . . . two steps . . . three. The steps were feeble and shaky, and the aide rushed to his support before the fourth step, but Bill had walked! Really walked!

It was an awe-ful moment.

Of course, many long, tedious months lay ahead while Bill tried to perfect his walking skill, but he was on his way!

I didn't spend long in rejoicing; in fact, realizing one problem was solved made me turn my attention to the problems that were not solved. How I longed for Bill's mental improvement! While he was at Green Valley, I had been so thrilled with his speaking at all and so worried about his moments of confusion that I hardly noticed even in his clear periods that he didn't actually converse with me. He spoke, for the most part, only isolated sentences. As soon as he came home and I saw him in the familiar setting, I must have subconsciously expected him to snap back to normal, and I expected we'd have long lively discussions spiced with his wit and humor.

One day I put a portable TV set in front of Bill and tuned in a talk show. He appeared to follow it, so when it was over I asked, "Do you agree with So-and-So's views?"

In prestroke days such a question might have started a discussion between us that went on for hours, but this time Bill answered with one word, "Partially."

"What don't you agree with?" I persisted.

"I'll tell you later," he answered.

"Later" never came.

Another day and another talk show, and I asked him, "What did you think of it?"

He answered, "It would take too long to tell you."

Also it grieved me that he never sang. The prestroke Bill had a beautiful and powerful baritone voice, and I was used to his singing any time from morning till night. He'd get up before I did in the mornings to make the coffee, and when it was time to wake me he'd begin singing. (Often his selection was, "Oh, How I Hate to Get Up in the Morning.")

Now about ninety per cent of the time he was listless and a bit vague; about five per cent of the time confused or even irrational; and five per cent as sharp and quick-witted as ever.

I tried to reason with myself: It's a blessing that he is still vague. He doesn't suffer the frustration, the humiliation, and the embarrassment he would suffer if he fully realized his state and how much the nurses and I have to do for him. It's a blessing, too, that he hasn't recovered physically before he has recovered mentally. Without the full use of his mind, he might, with physical ability, do many idiotic and dangerous things. I repeated to myself my friend Therese's words, "God's timing is always perfect."

Then I told myself: Since God has allowed this tremendous illness, surely it must win blessings for us here and hereafter. If Bill had never become ill and had later retired from business, would we ever have irritated each other. Would we have argued about money management or any other matter?

Never, never, never would we have been bored with each other, that's for sure. Every individual person is a mystery; every person unfolds as time goes by. Hence we would have kept on discovering more and more about each other and loving each other more. As Mark Twain wrote, "Love seems the swiftest, but it is the slowest of all growths. No man or woman really knows what perfect love is until he or she has been married a quarter of a century." So the longer Bill and I were together, the more interesting I found him. The prestroke Bill had his faults, but dullness was definitely not one of them. So often I'd say something, or there would be a line in a book presenting an idea, and he'd turn the idea around like a prism and show me a new facet of it. Or to change the metaphor, he made ideas expand and grow. To my way of thinking, everybody else by comparison seemed lackluster. And I know I was the companion he wanted; he used to say, "I'd rather be with my dear wife than with anybody else in the whole world," and shortly before the CVA he said, "I'm happier now than I've ever been in my life. It seems that every year of marriage gets better."

Although I can well understand why novelists and poets extol young love, I can't understand why they so often neglect richer and more satisfying older love. Young love is like a vine-covered cottage, picture-card pretty and heady with the perfume of flowers blooming round about it. Older love is like a fortress, weather-beaten, tough, hard, and so proud because it is all but impregnable to assault and so selfsufficient because it is a city unto itself.

Except for Bill's occasional business trips, my trips to see my family, or my trips in connection with my writing, we were never apart (unless my monthly Writers Guild meetings and his Shakespeare Club meetings count.)

On the other hand, we could flare up in anger at each other. Bill used to quote the Irishman who said, "Murder, yes; divorce, never."

Now, if the Blessed Mother persuaded her Son to cure Bill, I believed we would have something almost indescribably blissful, and the illness would serve a purpose. After coming this close to losing each other, surely we would be overwhelmed with gratitude for a second chance at marriage, and nothing, absolutely nothing, could ripple the waters of our domestic peace and joy.

How I longed for the next installment! Hoping to hurry mental recovery, I tried to find time to read to Bill, and as I had for months, I often played the Talking Book records. One day I was reading aloud a book I knew he had enjoyed in the past, and then I paused and asked him something about it.

He made no comment.

I would have felt even worse about this very uncharacteristic lack of response, if there had not been that five per cent sharpness. Another day that was evident. I was arguing with Bill, trying to get him to move his left hand, which he could do slightly but usually wouldn't do, and instead of arguing back, he recited from Alice in Wonderland:

> 'In my youth' said his father 'I took to the law,
> And argued each case with my wife;
> And the muscular strength which it gave to my jaw
> Has lasted the rest of my life.'

Whenever these flashes of the old Bill came, I yearned to put a book in his hands, but I worried and wondered if he would be able to read it. Came the day when I had to find out. I phoned an oculist whom we knew not only as a doctor but also as a co-member of Wyncote Players. Kind gentleman that he is, he agreed to make a house call. His conclusion after examining Bill was: "There's some sight still in the left eye." But he said the stroke had affected Bill's up and down sight, and he prescribed new glasses that he thought might enable Bill to read a little.

Once the glasses arrived, I summoned up my nerve, handed Bill a book and said, "Honey, I know you don't feel well, but can you read this?"

He answered, "Yes," and he sat there for some time with the book before him. I was all but biting my fingernails because I couldn't tell whether he actually was reading. Finally, I blurted out, "Read aloud to me."

He read the chapter title that was centered on the page, but when he began to read the text (haltingly), he read only the middle words on the page, that is he skipped both the beginning and the end of each line. Of course nothing he read made sense.

I was crushed — or is "crushed" too strong a word? I told myself: This is the first time he has read since the CVA. You can't expect perfection yet. His sight will improve. (It did. Eventually he read normally.)

Meanwhile his walking was improving every day, and he depended less and less upon the person who "walked" him. (By "walked him," I mean supported him on his left side.) So the day came that the nurses and I, as well as the therapists, walked him. Mr. Cardelli now gave us orders; he said, "Pay no attention if he tells you he's tired. Walk him till *you* drop."

In years past Bill once had a serious business reversal, and he had commented, "It would be OK I guess if a person could only remember and truly believe that if he 'seek . . . first the kingdom of God, and his justice, all these things shall be added unto' . . . him."[1]

I should have bound those words to my forehead as the ancient Hebrews bound scriptural texts to their foreheads in phylacteries. I did at least think of them sometimes when Bill had reversals in his recovery. His progress never went upward in a straight line for long; the pattern was usually three steps forward, one step backwards, but for the next couple of months it seemed more like three steps forward, two steps backwards.

Obviously there was *some* progress since the nurses and myself were now able to take him up and down stairs. We couldn't have done that if he hadn't helped himself considerably more than he did before. He would hold onto the banister with his strong right hand, lift his right foot to the next step, and then (sometimes with help) pull up his left foot.

There were frights and there were falls in the whole walking process. The first time I tried to take Bill from bed to bathroom, he leaned back and, try as I might, I couldn't hold him. I had to let him ease to the floor. He lay at my feet, and there was no way I could lift him any more than I could have lifted a ten-ton truck. Nor could he help himself up. I phoned my next door neighbor, Ray, and he came right over. He and his wife, Deana, were ultra-kind from start to finish, but that night I felt Ray was nothing less than a ministering angel. He managed to get Bill up.

Another time Gerry was taking Bill upstairs, and they had

reached the midway point when Bill said, "I'm too tired. I can't lift my foot one more time."

Butterflies the size of eagles fluttered in my stomach, but Gerry, smiling as always, said in that bright, lilting voice of hers, "Suit yourself," and she eased him down to a sitting position on a step. Then she turned to me and said, "I think your husband might like a cup of coffee and some cookies. It's about time for a break."

I made the coffee while she stayed with Bill. After his little snack, he was willing to try the stairs again. I sighed with relief when we got him to the second floor. Climbing Mt. Everest could not have seemed to me a greater achievement.

The first time I tried to get Bill upstairs alone was more frightening. I told Gerry, "I've got to do it eventually. There will come a day when no nurse will be around, and I'll be on my own. You just stand close by in case I run into trouble, but don't help unless you have to."

Our stairs go down to a landing and then branch, with two steps into the kitchen and two steps into the living room. I got Bill up the two steps, and he was resting on the landing, his right hand holding the newel post, and Gerry was congratulating me, "You're great."

Then I tried to turn Bill toward the main flight of stairs and get his right hand from the post onto the banister. I will never know exactly what happened, but his hand must have slipped off the post and failed to grasp the banister; anyway, Bill spun around with his back toward the living room and began to fall. Frantically, I grabbed for him but couldn't hold him. Gerry somehow managed to catch his legs, or his knees, or . . . and broke his fall. Nonetheless he went down all the way, with his head in the living room and his feet on the landing, while his body spanned the two steps.

Good old Gerry! She pulled him by the shoulders into the living room so that he was lying full length on the floor and said to him, "You can rest a bit before we take you upstairs." Then she went back to the kitchen and made *me* a cup of coffee.

I'll admit I was shaking. Bill could have broken his back, or a leg, or a hip. As it was, he wasn't even bruised.

It was the next fall that was nearly disastrous. I took Bill all the way up the stairs to the last step, and then he seemed to lean backwards. Terrified that I couldn't hold him and that he would tumble all the way down the entire flight, I instinctively gave him a shove forward. He crashed down onto the floor of the upstairs hall.

He complained that his side hurt, and when it came time for the passive exercises, he protested that he couldn't endure the pain. Thinking he was looking for an excuse to dodge the hated ritual, Gerry and I went merrily ahead moving his left arm and leg, and it was only when he said, "I'd rather die than have those exercises again," that I woke up and arranged for X-rays. To my horror they showed a broken rib and a tiny hairline fracture in the radial head of the left elbow.

Neither needed any setting of bones or surgery, but I was appalled at the exquisite torture we must have inflicted on Bill by moving his left arm.

There were other falls though none that bad. Three times we had to phone the police to get Bill up. (Incidentally, they always came very promptly and were very kind.)

Once Gerry and I were both in the living room not more than a few feet away from Bill as he sat watching TV. It never occured to us that he could stand up by himself, but that day he did it and instantly, before either of us could get to him, sank to the floor. No harm done that time, thank God.

Afterwards we put him only in a deepseated upholstered chair that we figured he'd need a crane to pull himself out of. Nonetheless, when I was alone in the house with him (to cut expenses I had less nursing care than ever by this time) and had to go to the kitchen to prepare a meal, I was always peeking in the door to make sure he hadn't stirred. There was no use saying, "Honey, don't move till I get back," because he wouldn't remember what I'd said.

One evening I left Bill for seconds only sitting in his wheel chair in the sick room, and I heard a noise. I ran back to him to see what could have made a sound and — was it an optical illusion? — I found Bill sitting on the bed. When I got my voice, I gasped, "How did you get there?"

"Walked," Bill answered, as calm as custard.

The distance between chair and bed was about two or three feet so he had taken a couple of steps on his own. Whenever he had taken such "free steps," as Mr. Cardelli called them, they had always been when a therapist was walking him and then gradually let go.

The chair-to-bed move seemed at least a mini-miracle especially since a day or so before when I had been putting him to bed and I had asked him to take one step *with my help* and support toward the bed, he didn't do it. I couldn't hold him up indefinitely, so I had to give him a push toward the bed. Then I said impatiently, "Oh Bill, what's the matter with you? Why didn't you take one step?"

He answered, "I don't know. I couldn't. It was as though my left leg were paralyzed."

I told Mr. Cardelli about the two instances and he, like the Green Valley Director, used the analogy of wires — but differently. The Director had said, "Some of the wires to the brain have been destroyed." Mr. Cardelli said, "There are loose wires. Sometimes they make connection with the brain. Sometimes they don't."

Although the Director was undoubtedly right about some "wires" being destroyed, I'm sure Mr. Cardelli was also right about others being merely loose (or damaged) and hence capable of making occasional connection. Bill's reasoning power faded in and out. Page after page of my diary laments that he no longer discussed ideas and opinions with me. At most, he conversed about factual matters, and the one bright spot was that these conversations sometimes showed penetrating intelligence. One such conversation that I typed up for my diary went like this:

Bill: "I had a stroke didn't I? A massive one?"

Me: "Yes, honey, you know you did. I told you about it. It was actually a cerebral hemorrhage caused by the rupture of an aneurysm."

Bill: "That kind of stroke is like a bullet in the head. It suffuses the brain with blood and destroys a certain number of brain-cells. The damage is permanent."

Me: "Oh no! Not necessarily permanent." (I was still hoping for a maxi-miracle.)

Bill: "With a severe stroke there is some permanent damage. You can't tell at first how much, nor its exact nature. It can be very serious and usually is. A stroke affects different people different ways."

Me: "I'm convinced that in your case there will be no permanent damage, great or small."

Bill: "I hope you're right, but I know my brain isn't working on all cylinders now. I'm not alert. I'm in a haze all the time."

Me: "You'll be all right. It takes time to get over what you've been through."

As we spoke, I was filled with conflicting emotions: amazed happiness that his mind was working so well as to understand his condition; compassion that he understood so well and would then mentally suffer the more; glad again that he didn't and couldn't hold a thought long and so wouldn't continue indefinitely to be aware of his condition.

Another aware moment came the day I said to him, "You always had a 'bring on your wild cats' attitude. With your determination, you will soon learn to walk alone."

He answered, "I think one of the effects of this disease must be to change your personality."

Medical opinion would have agreed with him. I had heard his very words from nurses and doctors. But I asked, "What do you mean? How has the disease changed you?"

"Well," he said slowly, "it seems to have sapped my spirit. It's made me apathetic."

How right he was! But again I was filled with conflicting thoughts and emotions. While tears of pity stung my eyes, at the same time a part of me was shouting "Hurrah!" for Bill's clear discernment. His remark had showed the old perceptive Bill. And I kept wondering if or how I could get him to think clearly more often.

Just about then a good friend in Wyncote Players, Barbara, had begun to come over every Tuesday to read to Bill. After that, for four years on end, she rarely, if ever, missed a Tuesday. (Her kindness deserves, but I fear won't get, a whole chapter.) She read everything from history to humor, and she would ask Bill questions about the reading and prod him to answer.

I was thrilled as I watched her in action. On the first day she read familiar passages from Shakespeare and then asked Bill to go on with the quotation. He did— and for six, or eight, or more lines.

Later, in a rash and exuberant moment, I wrote several friends saying that the brain damage probably wasn't permanent. One friend made one hundred Xerox copies of my letter, and the missive went from Maine to Louisiana. But later, in calmer moments, I realized that unless we had our miracle, some damage was indeed permanent. Meantime, in hopes of activating his mind further, I decided he needed to get out and see new sights.

If it were to be done, Cardelli and/or his aides would have to get Bill in and out of the car each time. Mr.Cardelli put me off for a short time, but the day to implement my idea did come.

On our first expedition I drove to a church, parked at a side-entrance where there were no steps, and the aide got Bill out of the car and into the building. It was about 3 P.M. on a weekday so nobody was there. I told Bill "Say a prayer of thanksgiving that the good Lord saved your life, and ask for a complete cure."

Some friends, hearing of Bill's outing, invited us over for a visit. Bill certainly wasn't his old scintillating self on that first social call, but he gave us all, particularly the attendant aide, one good laugh. Our host had asked about Mr.Cardelli, and Bill answered, "He's an egomaniac."

Nobody in that room or elsewhere could have given a more

accurate or a more succinct surface description of the man. Although I believe that basically Mr. Cardelli was, and is, humble because he credits God for his feats, listening to his oft-repeated, absurd statement, "I'm the best therapist in the world," (to which Bill usually responded, "Do you know all the therapists in the world?") a stranger might easily label Cardelli "egomaniac."

After that social sortie, undaunted Gerry took the attitude, "Anything you can do, I can do better," and she didn't see why she alone couldn't do what the therapist had done, get Bill in and out of the car — and she did. A week or so later, when Joe and Jeanne came up for their next visit (in November) we decided we could safely take Bill for the first time to our own church for Mass. The building has steps, but we got Bill up them easily.

Our pastor said from the pulpit, "Many of you may know that one of our parishioners suffered a massive stroke almost exactly one year ago today. He has made a remarkable recovery, and he is here this morning. His family wish to thank you for your prayers and ask you to continue praying for further recovery."

I looked around and some of the parishioners were actually crying.

Now that the ice was broken, I often took Bill to Sunday Mass when I had a nurse with me. One Sunday, after we went, a kind generous friend sent over a note saying what an "inspiration" it was to see us at Mass, and to show her "admiration," she was sending "a small gift." The gift turned out to be some high-quality liquor. Although Bill wasn't a drinker himself, it pleased him that I should have the best, and he spoke up with a pre-stroke sort of facetious quip, "With those results, we'll have to go to Mass every Sunday."

But Sunday is but one day of the week. I began to take Bill out almost daily, or whenever I had either a nurse or a therapist to help with the in-and-out-of-the-car business. Ever since I had mastered walking Bill up and down stairs, I had, for economic reasons, even more drastically cut back on nursing care. Virginia, Marcella, and Hugh had found full-time jobs elsewhere, but Gerry, who had small children at home, was content to work part time. Also fairly frequently, I had two other excellent nurses, Mary and Louise, willing to come in for just an hour or two.

On our jaunts we sometimes went to the public library to walk Bill through its familiar doors. Other times we took him to Wyncote Players shows (and to its annual banquet), to a small cocktail party hosted by old friends, in short to any place where he'd meet people and have that desired "mental stimulation." Gerry and I felt we were world travelers when we drove him into town (Philadelphia) to visit his old office. A couple of men met us at the door to help Gerry get Bill inside and into the elevator while I parked the car. That day Bill held court. The office force came by one by one to greet him. The girls kissed him and made a big fuss over him. The men gave him bear-hugs or slaps on the back and told him jokes they said they'd been saving for him. Unfortunately, he didn't respond with jokes of his own. In prestroke days, he had had an almost endless reportory because, he explained, "I'm like Irvin S.Cobb who said he 'had a good memory and hoped that nobody else did.'" Our grandson, Billy, once declared, "Granddaddy, you must have them written on the inside of your glasses. You couldn't remember them all."

With this gadding, naturally I discontinued home therapy and instead took Bill as an out-patient twice a week to St. Thomas Hospital. The bicycle machine, the electric vibrator, and other equipment there were a help, but above all at the hospital Bill had more of Mr.Cardelli's personal therapy than he had with house calls.

Only on St.Thomas-going days did Gerry come for an eight-hour shift, arriving in midmorning. Then followed a schedule that worked with the precision of a count down for a rocket launching:

10:30 Bathe and shave Bill
11:00 Give him passive exercises
11:30 Lunch

12:00 Put Bill to bed for short nap
 1:00 Get Bill up and dress him
 1:30 Get Bill into car and drive to hospital
 2:00 Arrive at hospital

Sometimes I'd drop Bill and Gerry there and go to a supermarket or some store, returning to pick them up at 5:30. Not that Mr. Cardelli worked with Bill over three hours on end. He would work with Bill and alternately with several other patients ten or fifteen minutes each at a time, so Bill had intervals of rest and of treatments on the various machines administered by aides.

Once at home, the schedule was almost as rigid.

 6:00 Gerry put Bill to bed for a short nap while I got dinner
 7:00 Gerry having left, I got Bill up and served dinner
 8:00 Put Bill to bed
 8:30 Loaded dishwasher, sorted laundry, and sometimes, if I
       had enough energy left, made out checks to pay bills.

The St. Thomas therapy speeded up progress. Soon Bill took "free" steps at home while Gerry walked beside him, alert to give him a steadying hand if he needed it. In fairly short order, I followed suit.

Mr. Cardelli said, "Bill could walk alone now, as long as he has a cane. He has all the pieces. He just doesn't, or can't, put them all together."

And he didn't for a while. Again, what the doctors and nurses called a "plateau!"

One December Sunday a Mass reading was from St. James "Be patient therefore, brethren, until the coming of the Lord. Behold, the husbandman waiteth for the precious fruit of the earth; patiently bearing till he receive the early and latter *rain*."[2]

Maybe that was what the Lord was asking of me, patience and more patience. He would have to help me acquire it too. ". . . without me you can do nothing."[3]

{10}

The kindness of family and friends at Christmas warmed me through and through. The house, filled with gifts of red poinsettias, looked like a florist shop, and we received enough fruit, cookies, liquor, and other fancy foods to wine and dine the 82nd Air Borne. The nurses brought us a tree and decorated it with twinkling lights and shiny ornaments.

But once Christmas passed, gloom descended as though someone had drawn all the blinds. With the grim winter weather, we could rarely get Bill out— not even to St. Thomas. The nurses and I did what we could walking him in the house and, abetted by Mr. Cardelli, we waged a campaign to force Bill to use his left hand. He moved it, but he never tried to use it. When I put a cookie in his left hand, he would immediately switch the cookie to his right hand. Then, if I grabbed it and said, "Oh no! You must use your left hand if you want that cookie," his response was, "To hell with it."

It was a losing battle.

The months of January, February, and March can be lumped together and described in one word, "woeful." I felt we were all but drowning in a sea of misery. Prayer was the rock I clung to, and the prayer was embedded in the scriptural verses that I read in the daily Mass prayers of my old Missal. I wrote many of them in my diary:

"I have cried to the Lord with my voice: and he hath heard me from his holy hill."[1] In parenthesis I commented ("Surely, the Lord heard me. Why is He holding off?")

"I have heard thy prayer, and I have seen thy tears, behold I will add to thy days fifteen years:"[2] ("Oh, if the Lord would only give Bill fifteen more years! Healthy years. Or ten years. Or five.

If He would only even things up by lopping years from my life and adding them onto Bill's so that the two of us would come out even with the same life span! A few more normal years together, oh God, please!")

"And the servant was healed at the same hour."[3] ("Healed! Maybe Bill and I will wake up and find that the stroke faded with the dawn like a nightmare because Christ has healed.")

"For the whelps also eat of the crumbs that fall from the table of their masters."[4] ("Oh, maybe Bill and I don't deserve a full meal, but give us, oh Lord, at least some more crumbs — some more miracle-installments.")

We had to wait until spring for a crumb or a miracle-installment. That was when I learned to get Bill in and out of the car by myself. Doing this not only meant that Bill was helping himself more; it meant that we were no longer prisoners in the house when no nurse was with us. A doctor-friend said to me, "Now you've really had your miracle! This didn't seem possible. The case is one for the medical journals."

Maybe we had had many miracles, and I hope I was not ungrateful, but if Bill were ever to be cured completely, we needed as many miracles again — or else one biggy.

As time went on I seemed to sorrow more, not less, about his brain damage, and the loss of his old-style conversation and companionship was like a hidden and painful ache that I carried around with me. Before the stroke I used to tell him once in a while, "You're a Renaissance man. You're up on everything from symphonic music to football, from Shakespeare to nonsense verse, from ancient history to jokes going the office rounds, but that has its drawbacks. If you'd only stick to one thing instead of spreading yourself all over the map, you could be a VIP specialist."

Yet it was his all-roundedness that made him such a fascinating (to me) life partner. He used to be interested in my writing, too. About this time I wrote a couple of short pieces, read them to him, and asked his opinion. About one, he said, "It's good." About the other, "It's boring."

Mere comment, not criticism! I wanted a discussion analyzing what the articles said and how well they said it. His two words seemed utterly worthless; they didn't point out any flaws that I could correct. Strangely though, the article he called "good" sold first time out; the one he called "boring" never sold at all though I sent it hither and yon. Maybe his mind was working better than I thought it was, but he had found it an effort to give me specific criticism. I was always beset by uncertainties of this kind. I was always wondering just how much he understood.

Incidentally, I did almost no professional writing during those days. A friend said, "There certainly is a contrast between your past and present lifestyles. I remember when you wrote *Mister Music Maker*, you went to California to stay at Lawrence Welk's home, and you went to the inaugural balls with his party and all. I remember Virginia Knauer taking you to the White House when you interviewed her, and you flew a helicopter when you wrote that article about the aviation pioneer Harold Pitcairn for *Suburban Life*."

Truthfully, I didn't have time to miss that part of my life, or if I did, I considered it inextricably bound up with the old life-with-Bill. Since he was now ill, it seemed natural for it to collapse along with everything else. I was mildly surprised that the earth continued to rotate on its axis.

What distressed me at this stage was the fact that Bill's progress, as far as I could see, was just about nil. I said so to Marcella one day when she substituted a few hours. She answered, "Haven't the doctors explained to you that patients of this sort reach a permanent plateau?"

I don't remember what I replied, but I wrote in my diary, "That hated word 'plateau' again! Of course doctors have told me that *naturally* there's no hope of Bill's climbing any higher, and my answer is the same as it has always been: I believe and accept the fact that you've done everything you can *naturally* so now I am banking on the *supernatural*. The power of the best doctor is limited. The power of prayer is unlimited because it draws on the omnipotence of God."

Well, both Marcella and I were off base. Contrary to Marcella's expectations, Bill moved from the plateau, and contrary to my expectations, he moved not up, but down.

August was a thirty-one day horror. First, I had word from Memphis that Katharine's husband, Paul, had developed cancer, and it was inoperable. He had perhaps a year to live.

While I was still reeling under this shock and wondering, as Katharine said, "how such dreadful things could have happened to both our husbands," that I became aware that Bill, for no apparent reason, had begun to slip— and mentally too. Like a person far advanced in senility, he would ask me a question such as, "Is this morning or afternoon?" and then ask that same question over and over perhaps fifteen or twenty times in an hour.

I was terrified. I felt as though we were in a car careening down a mountainside at 100 miles an hour, and neither of us knew how to put on the brakes. Jack, our G.P.doctor, said in effect, that there were no brakes; that nothing could be done. But Mr.Cardelli urged, "Get him to a specialist," and he suggested a certain neurosurgeon.

Tests in this doctor's office indicated a possible obstruction that inhibited the blood-flow to Bill's brain. The surgeon recommended hospitalizing Bill for an arteriogram (or an angiogram as it is also called). In this procedure, dye is injected into an artery that leads to the brain, and then the brain is x-rayed.

The surgeon admitted that there might be minimal danger in the arteriogram, but he said, "We do it hoping it will show us how to help the patient. If there is indeed an obstruction, the chances are we can remove it."

Brain surgery! I'd never sanction that— such was the thought that flashed across my mind, but I did OK the arteriogram, praying with Job, "dost thou uphold the arm of him that hast no strength?"[5] I felt utterly prostrate, and I could hope only that this would lead to the Promised Land where the cure awaited us.

The arteriogram showed that Bill had several enlarged occipital veins that could cause another stroke at any time. Also it showed that the main artery to the brain, the anterior vascular artery, instead of lying loose, was stretched tight in a curve indicating a swelling and pressure behind it that inhibited blood flow to the brain.

The surgeon proposed two operations: a "comparatively minor" one to remove the pressure on the main artery; the other "a more delicate procedure" to remove the enlarged veins. He told me to forget the more serious and delicate operation for the moment and concentrate on the first one. He called it a V.J. (ventrical jugular) shunt, a procedure often used in encephalitis. As he described it to me, it sounded as though he had taken the idea from a Rube Goldberg cartoon. He would bore a hole in the skull and insert, as a permanent fixture, a tiny pump to draw off the fluid that caused the swelling. The fluid would go into an artificial artery that he would insert in the neck by making an incision there. The new artery would return the fluid to the blood stream.

This was "comparatively minor!"

I gasped, "It has to be highly dangerous."

"Any operative procedure has some danger," said the surgeon, "but this one is not alarming, and it will make Mr. Coakley at least as keen mentally as he was before the retrogression — probably more so. We don't know how long this pressure has been building up. Perhaps since the day of the CVA."

"And if I don't OK the shunt? Will he retrogress further?"

"Most likely."

I knew that Bill, if he were able to speak for himself, would say, "If there's even the slightest chance of restoring brain function, what are we waiting for? Let's get the show the hell on the road."

Still I hesitated. It might jeopardize Bill's life. I told the surgeon that I wanted to discuss the operation with our son before I decided.

But then I had second thoughts about consulting Joe. If anything he said influenced me to have the shunt and Bill died, Joe would never forgive himself. Besides, he and Jeanne were vacationing in Puerto Rico, and I didn't want to ruin their holiday.

It was, as I saw it, up to me alone, so once again it was onto my knees. I prayed, "Oh Lord, show me what to do."

Also I made out a long list of questions to ask the surgeon. When I saw him again, I began with, "If I don't OK the shunt, is it certain that my husband will continue to regress mentally?"

He answered, "If you don't OK it, he will die in a month to six weeks."

I never asked another question. The Lord had showed me what to do.

{11}

Was Our Lady going to use the operation to cure Bill? When I asked myself that question, hope leaped up like a flame. At the heart of the flame though was fear— fear for Bill's life.

On the actual day I was as taut as strung wire. Promptly at 9 A.M. Bill was wheeled to the O.R. and I was left to wait. The operation was a four-hour job! And even when it was over, I couldn't see Bill pronto. He was taken into the Recovery Room. Maybe I couldn't have managed to sit still in the hospital lounge those edgy hours except that my loyal friend, Alberta, stayed with me throughout, and toward the last hour Jeanne arrived. (Jeanne had hardly unpacked from the Puerto Rican trip when my phone call had come announcing the operation, and she began repacking to fly North to lend Bill and me moral support. My ever-kind friend, Ruth, had met her at the airport and driven her to the hospital.)

When at last I did see Bill, he was unrecognizable as a live person, much less as himself. His head, most of his face, and his neck were swathed in bandages and his body was covered by sheets. I had to take it largely on faith that the inert bulk lying on the bed was really Bill.

The next morning a nurse tied his good right hand to the bed rail, saying, "Patients often try to pull at the bandages."

Bill's first words to me were, "They've got me bound up like a criminal. Please untie me."

"I can't," I answered.

"You can, but you won't," he said dryly.

Spoken like the old Bill! Jeanne and I looked at each other and grinned.

After that sweet and hopeful note, our usual soap-opera pattern called for a sour note. It came in the form of confusion and listlessness. Bill didn't seem to know Jeanne, and he didn't remember how many grandchildren we had.

The surgeon shrugged that off, saying, "Some people bounce right back when the pressure is relieved. Others take longer. This case may take three weeks."

Just the evening before, the evening of Operation-Day, he had told Jeanne and me, "You'll be surprised at how quickly Mr. Coakley bounces back. There will be marked improvement before he leaves the hospital."

This, I took to mean marked improvement in two weeks or less.

Then, because Bill was physically weak and almost helpless, the surgeon kept extending the estimate. "It could take weeks, even months." And finally he said, "It could be six months."

Six months! My fevered imagination saw Bill bedridden and inactive all that time, and my heart sank like a stone. If Bill were inactive for six months, the backbreaking therapy of the last year and a half would be cancelled out. We would have to begin again from scratch. How could Bill take it? How could I take it? Could I again push him to go through that torture?

The words of the prophet Samuel which I had read that morning, "The cords of hell compassed me"[1] . . . . echoed in my mind, and almost hysterically I begged the surgeon, "Please arrange for some therapy right now at this hospital. Bill mustn't forget how to walk."

A day or so later Bill was wheeled down to P.T., and in a few minutes I followed to see how the strange therapists worked. They had Bill on a table, and they were giving him passive range-of-motion exercises by moving his arms and legs. Then two of them stood him. Apparently he could no longer walk, but instead of using the foot-lifting tenchique, they more or less dragged him forward a yard or two, while he sagged between them like a half-empty burlap bag.

I burst into tears.

I asked the surgeon later, "What has the shunt done for my husband?"

"Saved his life," was the answer.

I almost asked, "For what?" Bill seemed as helpless as when he came from Green Valley many long months before, and as for his mental state — well, it was unstable. I reminded the surgeon "You practically guaranteed a quick recovery when you first proposed the shunt, and you said flatly that Mr. Coakley would be at least as keen mentally as he was before he regressed."

"I hope he will be, but nobody can guarantee anything. Wait and see. No doubt there will be improvement."

Wait, wait, wait — on a bed of nails.

When Bill was ready for discharge from the hospital, he was somewhat stronger but still not as strong as he was before he went in. In fact, his weak state meant I couldn't transfer him from bed to wheelchair solo, and (the insurance money having now been used up) I could no longer afford two full shifts of nurses. The most practical alternative seemed a nursing home; in such a place Bill would have the care of floor nurses. Happily, I could get Bill into the Hill House where Mr. Cardelli supervised the therapy. The "Big Boss" came there to walk Bill himself, and he gave orders to the resident therapists that they walk Bill twice a day.

The Cardelli-directed regimen did wonders, and soon I could laugh at the surgeon's six-months guesstimate that had so appalled me. In about a month, I could write in my diary, "Bill's walking is as good as it has ever been since the stroke."

Then I brought him home — and not by ambulance as he had arrived at Hill House, but in our friend Frank's car. When we reached the Coakley doorstep, Frank and I managed without ado to get Bill into the house and upstairs to bed.

I had heard of a Spanish-speaking woman, Alicia, newly arrived from Chile, who was looking for a job. I had not only studied Spanish, but I had been to both Spain and Mexico several times, so with a few gestures, and a handy dictionary, I could "speak" the language. I hired Alicia to help me with Bill and with *todas tareas domésticas*. Thus for less money than I would have paid nurses, I had someone all day long to help me bathe Bill, walk him, do the exercises, *and* the housework. The house was better kept than at any time since prestroke days. The only snag was that Bill could understand little of Alicia's Spanish, or of her heavily accented English, so he objected to being left alone with her even for a half hour. Finally, I decided to save up essential errands for Alicia's day off, and then I arranged for one of the nurses we had formerly had (mostly Gerry) to come in for the time it would take me to go to the supermarket, the library, the bank and so on.

Soon Bill seemed to be walking *better* than he had before the operation. The mental rebound wasn't as rapid as the physical, and that fact often had me in tears. On Thanksgiving day I opened *The Following of Christ*, and my eyes fell on the words, "Be thankful for the least blessing and you will be worthy to receive the greater."

Hastily, I murmured a thank-you prayer for Bill's walking prowess. I was indeed grateful, but it seemed that there was always something to roil the waters. A day or so later, Bill's regular doctor said, "It's possible that the hydro-encephalitis condition that caused the swelling and required the shunt was not related to the CVA. We simply are not sure."

Somehow, even the remote possibility that Bill's latest disorder was a separate thing from the CVA horrified me. It was, I felt, adding an *extra* burden to the already monstrous pile.

A talk with the neurosurgeon was more horrifying. I asked, "Exactly what are these pills you've prescribed for Bill?"

He answered matter-of-factly, "They're an anticonvulsant," and then explained that anybody with brain damage is prone to convulsions.

When I got my breath after that shocker, I told him, "I've never seen a convulsion. What'll I do if Bill gets one?"

The surgeon answered that Bill would "shake violently and probably fall." In any event, the doctor instructed me, "Put him down on the floor and roll him onto his side. Then put something hard like a tablespoon between his teeth for him to bite on."

At that moment, I think I was shaking violently myself. Now, added to fear of another stroke was the fear of convulsions, and then came a third fear: the pump in Bill's head, the doctor said, might have to be replaced at intervals of every few years.

I felt like a child in a black forest at night with hidden terrors leering at me from the shadows on all sides. Or I felt like I was walking a tight rope over a snake pit; I dared not look down at the dangers. Perhaps the second simile is better because I did try to keep looking up— up to God. If I hadn't, I might have fallen or had some sort of nervous collapse. I continually cried out silently, "God help us! I'm scared."

One day Bill asked about the pills, and above all I didn't want him to be frightened too about possible convulsions; on the other hand, Bill used to say I was "a lousy liar." My heart rose in my throat as I tried to appear to answer his questions without being informative. Afterwards I recorded the conversation in my diary:

Bill: "What are these pills?"
Me: "A prescription."
Bill: "Yes, of course, but what's in the prescription?"
Me: "Dilantin."
Bill: "What's that for?"
Me: "To dilate the blood vessels that go to the brain."
Bill: "Why do that?"
Me: "To get more blood to the brain."
Bill: "Why?"
Me: "The doctor thinks it's important."
Bill: "Did you ask the doctor why?"
Me: "Yes, but I didn't understand the explanation."
Bill: "What was the explanation? Maybe I'd understand it."
Me: "I don't remember. I can never remember things I don't understand."
Bill: "You'd have a bad time memorizing 'Jabberwocky.'" (He was referring to the poem in *Through the Looking Glass*.)

Then because Bill's mind was hazy and his memory so poor, he immediately began the conversation all over again by asking, "What are these pills?", and we stepped onto what I called a "merry-go-round conversation," repeating almost word for word what we had said the first time.

I couldn't see that the shunt made his mind function better. Oh certainly, there were occasional flashes of sharp intelligence, but there had been those from the first. Now, as before, I recorded each in my journal. One day I spoke of a "morganistic" marriage, and instantly Bill said, "You mean a morganatic marriage."

My mistake! Of course he was right.

Then one night as I was putting him to bed, I said aloud for "night prayers," the Hail Mary. I mumbled its last petition and Bill commented, "You slurred the 'and' so badly that it sounded as though you left it out and said, 'Pray for us sinners now at the hour of our death.' It's news to me that we're dying this instant."

At Mass on a Sunday, a young, visiting priest (not our pastor) preached and in the course of his sermon, urged us, his listeners, not to blame have-nots for fighting haves, and he said that equal distribution of wealth was a panacea for social ills. I didn't think Bill was taking it in at all until he turned to me and said, "That priest suffers from the liberal psychosis. He thinks material poverty causes all the world's ills."

Although these rare flashes were not indicative of consistent mental improvement, something did happen to Bill mentally after the shunt. He became cantankerous and uncooperative. I would take him to the bathroom door and, despite cajolery, persuasion and threats, he would refuse to go in so that Alicia and I could shave or bathe him or help him clean his teeth. One morning I actually took him to the bathroom door eleven times before he agreed to step over the sill. I couldn't push or pull him lest he lose his ever-precarious balance and fall.

If I tried to do anything for him, he would flare up and say angrily, "I'll do it myself," although it might be something like tie his shoelaces or file his nails which he couldn't possibly do alone. (He still didn't use his left hand.)

My friend Marie kept insisting, "This shows mental improvement. Of course he hates you to tend him like a baby. That humiliates him. When you did it at first, he didn't fully realize the invasion of his privacy. Now he does."

Bill had always been the sort of person who highly valued privacy, but at the time I was (besides being frustrated at his noncooperation) so appalled by his uncharacteristic bad humor that I couldn't see anything clearly. To me, it seemed as though Bill had turned into a stranger. Years before, after he had begun to believe in God, he had said, "A believer can't be grumpy. He's received the 'good news'! He knows where he is headed — it's heavenward. That's exciting. It makes him feel like shouting 'Hurrah'! three times every morning before breakfast."

In short, though Bill had his low moments, he used to come close to St.Paul's formula of "always rejoicing," and now it seemed he was coming close to always protesting, and I was too shocked by the switch to figure out why.

Then, of course, he no longer thanked me for small services as he had been doing previously, and this seemed another about face. Indeed, in prestroke days he was big on gratitude. After dinner he often said a complimentary word about the meal. I could fix a bland, uninteresting poached egg for breakfast or a homely grilled hamburger for dinner, and each time he'd probably say, "Great meal!" When we had guests, he often rather embarrassed me by praising the meal before they had a chance to comment — if indeed they were so minded. When I would remonstrate with him about this later, he'd laugh and say, "Can I help it if they're slow?"

You could no more squelch Bill Coakley than you could take the fizz out of newly-opened champagne. He effervesced. And now nothing I cooked seemed to please him much.

Would psychiatry help? It occurred to me that it might, and more important it might help stimulate his thought processes. (I still ached for his old-time companionship.)

After five or six sessions with Bill, a psychiatrist said, "Mr. Coakley is suffering from depression because he is vaguely aware of his condition. Moreover, he is furiously angry with himself because he cannot function normally, and he doesn't fully understand why. He takes out his self-anger on you because you are the nearest person. He is humiliated that you are waiting on him."

I could have saved the psychiatrist's steep fee, not only because I had Marie's similar diagnosis, but because for some strange reason I was too dense to assimilate what the man said. First of all, I had never had any experience with the kind of depression he meant (psychotic depression?) and I didn't know what it was. And then depression *and Bill!* Never the twain would meet in my mind. I continued to be incredibly obtuse, and hence Bill's crossgrained attitude continued to sandpaper my nerves. Once, dismay, disappointment, frustration, and rage all ganged up on me, and right in front of Bill I burst into tears. (From the beginning, I had made every effort never to let him see me cry, but this time I lost control.) Furthermore, I lashed out, "You make my life unbearable."

Instantly, he was contrite. He said, "Darling, I'm sorry. I apologize. I don't want to make things hard for you. You know how much I love you."

"Well then, let's get this morning ritual of teeth and bath over with."

"OK," he answered, "I'll do it in five minutes."

But in five minutes, he said, "I can't. I'm too tired.

Formerly, friends had often commented about how patient I was in nursing Bill. It had seemed to me a silly remark. Why shouldn't I be patient? In fact, my compassion for him made anything else impossible. But now that was changed, and I found myself shouting at him in a shrill voice, audible, I fear, on the far side of the moon, "Look, this is the fifth time I've taken you to the bathroom. You've got to go in and do your teeth, do you hear?"

I was ashamed after these outbursts, and an overwhelming compassion for him would return briefly. Then I would go into a crying jag. Gerry, who still came fairly often to bathe Bill (Alicia stayed on a full-time daily basis only a few months), said,

"Maybe he's spoiled with all the attention he gets. Why don't you put him in a nursing home just for a few weeks. It might help him and you."

I agreed to list our name in three or four homes, but when one of them notified me soon afterwards of a vacancy, I said, "Give it to the next person on the list." I realized I could never part with Bill, even for a few weeks, unless there were a compelling reason. Besides, I felt that he particularly needed me at this stage because Mr. Cardelli had declared, "I have no more tricks. I've taught Bill all I can. Now it's up to you to keep him walking and exercising so he won't regress. Bring him to St. Thomas only for an occasional checkup."

With the stairs (thank God I hadn't sold the house), Bill got a fair amount of walking and exercise. Unfortunately though, I couldn't get him out in the car as often as before because there were times when he would refuse to let me dress him. Friends offered to call for us and help me take Bill to Mass on Sundays. Although I accepted these offers, I never knew until the last moment whether I'd be able to get Bill ready. I said more prayers at home, begging the Lord to make Bill cooperative about my dressing him, than I said after I got to church. With time out for all the coaxing, cajoling and arguing, the dressing process sometimes took two hours.

I thought it was vital to Bill's mental health for him to go out, so I was immensely grateful to another friend, semiretired (Bea C.'s husband) who often on weekdays took Bill out without my going along. Once I accepted the kind offer of still another man to help me take Bill to Wyncote Players' current show, and then, when I found myself in a tizzy trying to get him dressed, I called this friend to say I'd changed my mind about going. That's the only time I was so chicken hearted.

Evidently Bill got out and walked enough to keep improving. Six months after the shunt and two and a half years after the CVA, he walked upstairs for the first time completely by himself. It was one of the BIG firsts, and I felt it was another miracle-installment.

Gerry said, "Now that Bill is walking upstairs by himself, let's try something else. I think one reason he hates us to bathe him is that we put him on that perforated metal chair. Let's try getting him down into the tub. He can help himself enough for us to get him out. I'll take off a shoe and stocking, step into the tub with one foot and hold him on the left side."

That incomparable Gerry! She was always willing and anxious to try anything. Like the famous King Richard, she had the heart of a lion. Despite the fluttery feeling in the pit of my stomach as I helped her with the tub manoeuvre the first time, it worked. And the next time Gerry did a solo performance. (By this time Alicia, with regrets on my part and on hers, had had to quit entirely. Gerry came twice a week to bathe Bill, and Harriet, a nurse-friend of long standing, came once a week). Bill did vastly prefer the tub bath, and he liked the fact that we now handed him the washcloth, saying, "Wash yourself."

Some weeks later, he picked up a book from the table near his chair and apparently began to read it. For months, Barbara, when she came to read to him, had put a book in his hands and asked him to read a few lines, and he had done it competently, but this was the first time I saw him pick up a book on his own initiative. He held it before him and turned the pages at regular intervals as though he were following the text. After that he read every single day — and an appreciable part of every day. I wasn't sure how much he absorbed, and when I asked him to tell me what he was reading, he'd answer, "It would take too long to tell you," or "Honey, why don't you read it for yourself?"

My guess was that he absorbed little and soon forgot that; the book-in-hand was just the habit of a lifetime reasserting itself.

Still the "reading" and the other good signs were highly encouraging, and I wished and prayed more fervently than ever that Our Lady would give us a few more mircle-installments — or one complete miracle to end all miracles for us. We now seemed *so* near — and yet so far.

How I longed to speed things. I believe the Lord helps those who help themselves, or as St. Ignatius put it, I believe that one should "Pray as though everything depends on God, but work as though everything depends on you."

I practically lay awake at night trying to think of ways to work for Bill's recovery. One idea came to me through a feature story I had somehow managed to find time to write for the *Philadelphia Bulletin* about an interview I had with an acupuncturist. Why not try acupuncture for Bill? We had nothing to lose.

After five or six treatments however, Bill showed no improvement. It was just one more thing I felt I had to try on the principle of not leaving a stone unturned, but there was one interesting facet to the experiment. Although I hadn't asked the acupuncturist about Bill's mental state, he confirmed the psychiatrist's opinion. One day he said gratuitously, "Here's an angry man. He's angry with himself because he doesn't function as he used to and doesn't fully understand why. If he should ever be cross with you, don't get hurt. He's just venting his frustration."

I then told the acupuncturist about Bill's post-shunt cantankerousness and he said, more or less what Marie had said, "That shows improvement because it shows more awareness," and also like Marie and the psychiatrist he said, "He's suffering deep depression."

Although Bill didn't seem to have much sense of time, and although I avoided speaking in his hearing of the length of his illness, he knew it had lasted a long while, and one day he said, "I'm never going to get well, am I?"

A lump rose in my throat and it was hard to make my voice sound cheerful as I answered, "Oh honey! Of course you are!"

I didn't convince Bill.

Looking back I realize— and I am appalled that I continued to be so amazingly obtuse about his depression. It must have crushed him, and yet I casually brushed it aside. Marie, who had had some experience with this psychic condition, had said, "Most people don't understand it. There's nothing worse than depression." And she added, "I'd rather have any kind of physical illness, including a stroke like Bill's. Depression is martyrdom."

Even those words didn't penetrate.

One reason for my density, I suppose, was that I was concentrating so hard on remedies for Bill's physical illness and on stimulation for his mind that I couldn't think of anything else. To help his mental progress now became my overriding aim. I even considered grabbing for the straw of hypnosis, and, to find out what it would do, I used myself as a guinea pig and asked a hypnotist to hypnotize me. Though he tried, I didn't respond. I suppose I was too busy analyzing his every move and making mental notes to relax.

About this time, Jack, Bill's regular doctor, retired from practice, so I had to find a replacement. The new doctor, a G.P., disparaged hypnosis for Bill. Since I had had even less hope for it than I'd had for acupuncture, I dropped the idea.

I was back to Square One, the point I had come to so often since the stroke occurred: there is no human hope; "Our help is in the name of the Lord."[2] Somebody sent me a prayer that read, "Dear Blessed Mother, where there is no way, please make a way." I said it over and over.

The second operation that the neurosurgeon had recommended (the one to remove the enlarged veins that threatened a future stroke) had faded, not disappeared, from my mind. Like Scarlett O'Hara, I told myself, "I'll think about it tomorrow." I really couldn't think then of putting Bill through another horrendous ordeal.

Meanwhile, I was getting bad news from Memphis, and soon word came that Paul, after a year-long bout with cancer, had died.

Ordinarily, I would have gone South on the first available plane. However, Alicia, who no longer worked for me regularly, could not come to the house to stay with Bill just then. Gerry and the other nurses all considered an eight-hour shift the longest working period out of any twenty-four that they could take on.

A couple of months later, when Alicia and her husband, who incidentally spoke excellent English, could stay at the house with Bill for an extended weekend, I made the trip to get a glimpse of Katharine and of Jeanne and Joe in Nashville. When I returned in just four days, I had an experience with an emotional impact that I will remember until I am laid in my coffin. When I came in the front door, Bill looked up and saw me. Tears sprang to his eyes, and he fixed me with a gaze that said more earnestly than any words could have, "Love, love, love." Then, though it was an effort, he got to his feet and started to walk toward me, and I was, in that instant, across the room and in his arms. His cane clattered to the floor, and we clung to each other as two drowning people. For the first time since the stroke, Bill even managed to get his left arm around me. Finally, he spoke, "Darling, darling, don't ever leave me again."

"Oh, darling, I won't, I won't," I promised "I never will."

A few months later Bill began to complain of constantly being tired. He complained to me. He complained to the nurses. He complained to Deana, our next door neighbor who, out of sheer Christian kindness, now came several days a week to help me with Bill.

Then one day in April when Barbara had asked him to read, I commented, "He sounds hoarse."

As I spoke, I suddenly remembered that the week before when I was dressing Bill, he said, "My collar is too tight. It hurts my neck."

Then on a night when Marie and I took him to the Wyncote Players' play, he said, "Skip the tie." This was a switch; fastidious Bill had always insisted upon proper dress.

I began to put the pieces together when I noticed a slight swelling on the side of his neck. Probably it's nothing, I told myself, but anyway I'll take him to the doctor. After this man, a G.P., examined Bill, he said, "I can't diagnose the trouble. I think you should see a surgeon."

Surgeon! The word was like a coin dropped into a vending-machine; automatically out popped a question that I hadn't consciously thought through at all, "Could it be cancer?"

"I doubt it," said the doctor, "but it could be."

This exchange didn't take place in Bill's hearing, and nobody used the word "cancer" when he was present, but when I took him to a surgeon (*not* the man who performed the shunt) Bill himself asked the same question that I had. Chills ran up my backbone when the surgeon answered, "We're going to hospitalize you for a biopsy and find out."

I phoned Tennessee and Joe, ever loyal, ever generous, flew right up.

The verdict came swift and definite as a karate chop: Cancer.

Later, when I was calm enough to talk it over with Joe, I remembered that back at Green Valley, doctors had said that the gastro-nasal tube (which had been threaded up Bill's nose and down his throat to feed him for almost seven months) "could cause serious throat irritation." I didn't remember to ask if the artificial artery which, since the shunt, ran from the head-pump down into and through Bill's throat, could also cause irritation. My first thought was: What can be done now?

The surgeon said, "I cannot operate."

"Is that because of the location of the growth, or because of my husband's general condition?"

"Both."

Probably the conversation wasn't very coherent from then on, but the gist of it was: "What about treatment?"

"I'll call in a chemotherapy specialist."

"How long do you expect Mr.Coakley to live?"

"I couldn't say."

"Couldn't you give me an idea? Six weeks? Six months? A year?"

"I don't think he will live a year."

"Will he be in great pain? Or will he choke to death rather than die of the cancer?"

"I don't think he will choke to death. I'm hoping the tumor will balloon outward, not inward."

The chemotherapy doctor vetoed treatments for Bill, and the surgeon then as much as told me to take Bill home from the hospital and wait for death.

I was beyond crying. I was even beyond speech. I walked away from the doctor without a word.

That night, lying in bed, unable to sleep, the words, "no natural hope" ran through my mind. And then I sat bolt upright and said aloud, "What's new about that? There never has been any natural hope from the beginning. The only hope was — and is supernatural. Nothing has changed."

I stretched out in the bed again, thinking: It will be no harder for "God, the Father Almighty" to cure Bill of cancer-plus-stroke, than stroke alone. Now, oh now, dear Blessed Mother, I beg you, I beseech you, I implore you, ask your Son for a complete cure.

I had to keep believing, "Ask, and it shall be given you . . . ."[1] I had often mulled over that text. It meant surely that every prayer is answered, but it couldn't mean that you always receive the very thing you ask for. God doesn't behave like a genie or a fairy godmother who always grants the three magic wishes even if they hurt or harm you. God answers prayer by granting you *a* favor, even if it isn't *the* favor you ask for. He gives you a boon if you should ask for a bane. A boon for Bill might mean death and Heaven. I had to face that.

Maybe I was like a kid who begs for the coffee he sees grownups drinking. His mother says, "No," and then gives the child lemonade that is better for him and that he really likes better.

It all made sense, but the trouble with these religious ideas was that (although they definitely nourished me and I couldn't have subsisted without them) they didn't stick in my mind. What I said before of gospel verses was true also of them; they were like bread. I couldn't "eat" in one day enough for a week; I had to have a *daily* portion.

Writing in my diary, I expressed that same thought, but differently. I wrote, "I was watching a singer on TV who wore a dark sequinned dress. Sometimes the dress looked dull, but when she moved, sequins here and there caught the light and shone for a second like miniature suns. Occasionally, too, a spiritual truth that has been in my mind all along like a dull, unstimulating fact, will catch fire and I 'see' it and I am heartened, but only for an instant. Spiritual truth is something I have to remind myself of constantly. And I need it more than ever now. It alone keeps me from despair."

I had had Bill home hardly a week or two when I could see a startling change. He was already far weaker than he had been before the brief hospitalization. I was almost afraid to bring him downstairs in case I'd be unable to get him up again. (By this time of course Joe had had to return to Tennessee to his family and job, so I was often alone in the house with Bill). His "I'm too tired" to eat, to walk, to listen to records, became a refrain.

The tumor grew and grew; it seemed to bulge bigger even as I looked at it.

In my diary, I noted, "Bill says fifty times a day, 'What's this thing on my neck? I keep thinking cancer, cancer, cancer.' And then we have a verbal exchange that goes like this: I answer, 'The doctors says it's an undifferentiated tumor.' (One of the doctors did use that term.)

"'Undifferentiated tumor! That's like saying the doctors don't know what the hell it is,' Bill says."

The next entry in my journal was that Bill had called me in the middle of the night in considerable pain. I had to administer the pills that the surgeon had prescribed. He said that when Bill could no longer swallow the pills, he would give injections to deaden the pain.

Needless to say, my heart ached, and ached, and ached for him. What *could* I do?

Tossing in bed at night and agonizing over that question, at length I came up with one idea. There are two replicas of the original statue of Our Lady that stands in the shrine of Fatima, Portugal. These replicas are called "pilgrim statues," because they are taken to churches throughout the world for "novenas," or nine-day prayer periods. Ordinarily they are never taken into private homes, but I thought, since I had been praying to Our Lady under her title of Our Lady of Fatima, it might move her if one could be brought to our home for Bill to see. Maybe, noting that we honored her likeness, she would cure Bill once and for all the day her statue arrived.

After many phone calls and letters to a friend in New York, arrangements were actually made for the statue to be brought to our home for an hour's stay.

A change afterwards? Another miracle-installment?

Yes, at first there seemed to be a change, but it was for the *worse*. About twenty-four hours later, Bill choked so hard I thought he was going to stangle to death before my eyes.

101

He didn't, and the paroxysm passed, but Katharine who had flown up from Memphis, urged me, "Call the doctor."

Earlier in the day I had called the surgeon, and he had said that nothing could be done; in fact, he had added that Bill would probably live only a week or so since he was getting almost no liquid— much less solid food. Calling the regular doctor then seemed utterly useless to me, but at Katharine's insistence I did it anyhow.

He came immediately, and he was shocked to see how fast the tumor had grown and that it not only impeded swallowing, but it also interfered to some extent with breathing. He made three suggestions: a gastrostomy or a surgical opening into the stomach through which Bill could be fed; an operation to remove enough of the tumor to allow swallowing; or X-ray treatments. He said, "One of these might at least allow Mr. Coakley to die with less pain and anguish. I'll discuss my suggestions with the surgeon and get back to you just as soon as I possibly can."

The surgeon thought that the only suggestion with merit concerned the X-ray treatments, but he seemed to feel that Bill's chances of dying a less-than-excruciating death were just as good if we did nothing.

Again our pastor gave Bill the last rites of the Church. (This was at least the fourth or fifth time Bill had had them since the CVA.)

The regular doctor still believed that X-ray would obviate some suffering so he lost no time in arranging for me to take Bill to the hospital as an out-patient for a series of treatments.

The effect of the treatments was amazing— and amazingly rapid. They did more than obviate suffering; with dizzying speed they shrank the tumor completely and entirely. Soon Bill was eating and drinking as normally as the next person. I half-believed the tumor had been a figment of my imagination; it had come and gone so quickly.

But it was real enough, and I knew that if Katharine had not been there just at the crucial moment, if she had not urged me to call a doctor, and if the doctor had not acted so speedily, Bill would have been dead. I felt that the Blessed Mother had pulled the strings for all this to happen and had thus given us another miracle. (Maybe, she *was* pleased with our honoring her statue.)

In July, Jeanne and Joe came for a short visit, and by this time there was no sign of a tumor for them to see. Bill had indeed been given a reprieve, and while it lasted, there was always the hope of more miracles. We needed them. We were living with a time bomb; another tumor might appear and the X-ray doctor had made it very clear that Bill could tolerate no more treatments for two years. But we had lived with a variety of time bombs for so long that I had learned to shut my eyes to anything beyond the NOW, repeating, ". . . . Sufficient for the day is the evil thereof."[2]

Actually, in the next weeks Bill seemed to grow stronger than he had been in months. He walked about the house on his own quite freely, and I'm sure Jeanne and Joe went home vastly encouraged. However, one day shortly after they left, when Bill got to his feet, his left leg seemed to give way and he teetered. I jumped up, grabbed him by the shoulders and pressed my whole body against him, trying to keep him from pitching forward on his face. We lurched and swayed like two drunken dancers. I thought of the fireplace. If we should crash to the floor, Bill might hit his head with its pump-installation against the bricks. But somehow, after eons of anxiety, I was given the strength to force him backwards a step or so and down into his chair.

When the struggle was over, my heart was pounding so hard I felt it would break right through the wall of my chest.

In September he was still a little weaker, and one night I woke up and heard him groaning. I ran to him and asked, "What's the matter, honey?"

He answered, "Nothing."

"But you were groaning," I said.

"Well, I have a lot of pain."

Had the cancer metastisized and gone to another part of his body?

I forgot that dreadful thought the next day because of a trivial but to me ever-to-be-cherished incident. Bill and I were sitting in the living room across from one another on either side of the fireplace as we had done for years. Then Bill looked up from his book and over at me saying, "You're so pretty and sweet. It gives me joy just to look at you."

I felt as though he had punched a Wellsian time machine and rolled back the years. That was exactly and precisely the kind of thing he often used to say to me before the stroke. Tears sprang to my eyes. I believed— I KNEW — for that moment we actually did have a full and complete miracle! Bill was his old self.

The miracle belonged in the category of visions— blessedly beautiful but short-lived. Moreover, in another couple of months Bill was weaker again, and I found the words of St. Teresa of Avila running through my mind: "All things pass away, God only shall stay."

In November came the fourth anniversary of the CVA, and although Bill could now walk and talk, his death was as imminent as ever. On Thanksgiving day the fear of death enveloped me like a thick, black, suffocating cloud. I had cooked the traditional turkey, and I chopped up a little with gravy for Bill. He had been eating lightly but eating normally. That day he choked on the turkey and couldn't swallow it.

In the morning with trembling hand I dialed the surgeon's number and then that of the X-ray doctor. I told both men, "I think the tumor is returning."

When they examined Bill, they could find no evidence of it, but I was not reassured. I thought I could even detect a slight swelling on the other side of Bill's neck.

The first two or three weeks in Devember I remember as a blur of misery. Bill was choking over every mouthful of food, and on December twentieth, he choked so violently that Gerry and I feared strangulation and rushed him to the hospital by ambulance.

I was not only sure that it was another tumor, I was convinced more than ever that I could put my finger on the very spot that it lodged, on the side of his neck opposite that of the first tumor. Yet tests at the hospital proved inconclusive.

What next?

Since the doctors were giving Bill no treatment and declared they could give him no treatment, I suddenly realized that it was desperately important to me to have him home for Christmas even if he had to return to the hospital the very next day. But could I persuade the doctor to discharge him? Bill was still "under observation," and he was still choking over food. I planned how I would approach the doctor and made up a little diplomatic speech to use on him. Actually though, I don't know what I said when the time came; all I know is that to my intense gratification the doctor agreed to discharge Bill.

He came home on Christmas eve.

A friend asked me later, "How did you get through Christmas?", and I answered, "Honestly, the day was joyous. I was so happy, so grateful to have Bill at home with me and alive."

If only he didn't have to eat! A teaspoon of jello, a sip of milk, a bit of mashed banana, a taste of jarred baby-food— everything made him choke. The choice seemed to be choking or starvation.

By New Year's Eve Bill was literally eating nothing. I couldn't get even a half-teaspoon full of water or a sliver of ice into his mouth without that near-strangulation. I hated to phone the doctor on a holiday, and since I had been told that X-ray treatments were taboo for two years, I figured there was absolutely nothing he could do for Bill anyhow. Never did I feel more surely that our sole "help is in the name of the Lord."

Maybe the Lord sent our doctor-friend, Frank. He happened to drop in, and he urged, "Get hold of your doctor. He can at least put Bill on intravenous feedings. They won't keep him alive long, but they'll insure that he will have less agony than if he dies of dehydration."

So, once more it was back to the hospital for Bill. The tests taken during this stay indeed showed a new tumor just where I had first suspected it was. It did not grow outward to the extent of the first tumor but was far more inward and was pressing on the esophagus.

After the I.V. was started up, there seemed nothing to do but wait for death. The next few days I spent nearly all my waking hours at the hospital sitting by Bill's bed with my rosary in my hands, clutching it till it made marks on my palms, but unable to say it or to pray verbally at all.

Then one morning when I went into his room, the bed was empty.

What had happened? Not death! I ran to the nurses' station and began spewing questions.

"He has been taken to the X-ray Department," the head nurse told me. "Doctor's orders."

I flew down the hall to the elevator that would take me to the X-ray Department too. The doctor in charge there told me that he had reconsidered and had decided that the second tumor was far enough away from the first to allow a few treatments after all. This way, he thought Bill would have a less painful death. "In other words," he said, "the treatments are merely palliative."

After the treatments Bill bounced back like a rubber ball. Another miracle? Anyway, he was soon discharged from the hospital, looking and feeling much better— and eating soft foods.

Although the doctor cautioned me to keep Bill upstairs, Mr. Cardelli came by and easily took Bill up and down. He thought it was safe for Gerry and me to do it too. When we did, we had no trouble; in fact Bill seemed to grow stronger every day.

Jeanne, who (kind and supportive as always) had flown up for a visit, was astonished when she saw his agility.

"Well," said Gerry, "what did you expect? This man is super human. I think he's going to live forever."

{13}

Yes, Bill did seem to get stronger. When he had left for Balfour Hospital, he was so weak that he had to be carried on a stretcher from a second-floor bedroom to the ambulance. A month later he walked up and down stairs by himself.

Chalk up one more miracle-installment?

No, not this time. Doctors explained that sometimes the good effects of X-ray treatments go on after the treatments themselves have ended. Apparently that is what had happened.

And the rally was mental as well as physical, so again there were flashes of the Bill personality. One day in late February I wrote in my diary that he said, "There's something unfair about our marriage . . . I got you, and you got only me."

Shortly after he made that quip, I had written a magazine article saying that my husband used to tell me all the time how great I was, how pretty, how dear, and the rest, but after he became ill, no more bouquets. I stopped bothering how I looked.

That theme that praise encourages a person to put on a shining face, is true enough, and one that I think is worth writing about, but the illustrations I used from our life were bogus, so later I regretted fictionalizing facts to make my point. Bill never even in his cantankerous periods entirely stopped complimenting me; he only did it less often.

Obviously, my account of the ups and downs of his illness would have to be true; not even a soap opera scripter could invent such an erratic seesaw.

After about two smooth months that almost lulled us into believing the cancer was cured, change came. Fatigue again. Weakness again. Then for the first time in his life, Bill complained, "I feel miserable," or "I've never felt so exhausted in my whole life," or "I've never been this sick before."

In prestroke days Bill rarely complained. I remember that I was furiously angry with him the actual day of the stroke because of his seeming bravado. When he crashed to the floor, I knew instantly: This is CATASTROPHE! I ran to him and pulled his head onto my lap. In the split-second before he became comatose, he said, "Don't worry, honey. I'm OK."

I could have shaken him and screamed, "Stop trying to be a hero."

But now over four years later, I didn't need his complaints to tell me that he was much worse. A third swelling bulged in his neck. The X-ray specialist said, and meant it this time, "No more treatments."

"It looks as though no road is open," I said to Bill's regular doctor the G.P. but he replied, "There's chemotherapy."

"Oh no!" That was my first reaction. Chemotherapy might poison the cancer cells, but it would poison healthy cells too and so produce painful side effects such as violent nausea. I couldn't bear to put Bill through one more thing— and for what? Without another miracle, chemotherapy would probably delay Bill's death for only a couple of months. I wanted a miracle without that added torture or, if no miracle, I was almost ready to say: Let him die in peace. Besides, right after the biopsy, a chemotherapist had vetoed that treatment for Bill.

Nonetheless the G.P. made an appointment for a chemotherapist to examine Bill. The date of the appointment was April second.

Working against that deadline, I tried to figure out meanwhile something less drastic to try. All through Bill's illness I read whatever I could lay my hands on about strokes and later about cancer. One of the books I read touted the alleged sometimes-cure for cancer, laetrile or B17, a substance derived from the chemical amygdalin found in apricot pits. At that time laetrile was banned in the United States (although it was used in many different countries and has since been legalized in twenty of our states) because the Federal Food and Drug Administration (FDA) had not sufficiently researched it and because it contains microscopic amounts of cyanide.

The nearest hospitals using it were in Canada and in Mexico. Bill couldn't have travelled ten miles, much less a thousand.

An organization in New York City which I phoned dispensed information, but not laetrile; that would have been illegal. I sent a cashier's check to Mexico and ordered some liquid laetrile for injections, to be sent me air-freight. A nurse, who occasionally had substituted for Gerry, said she had learned to give the injections in a London hospital. (They were not ordinary injections but the intravenous type that takes special training to administer.) She gave Bill exactly one injection, and then the next day told me she had qualms about it. Although the law did not usually concern itself with nurses but only with doctors who prescribed laetrile, it was possible that she could get into trouble.

What could I say? I couldn't urge her to continue with the shots. But I thought: Surely some doctor can and will do it. There's nothing immoral involved; laetrile is illegal simply because the FDA hasn't as yet compiled enough data either to endorse or to condemn it. Since, according to all medical opinion, Bill is going to die anyhow, why not try laetrile even if the chances of its curing him are only a thousand to one? Or a million to one? With similar odds people buy Irish sweepstakes tickets, and the prize is merely money, not life itself.

And maybe the chances are good. Who knows? The FDA doesn't. If laetrile works, the Blessed Mother may want to use this natural means of curing Bill for a dual purpose. A cure would certainly impel me to work overtime trying to lay the facts before the FDA, and Bill's case might then open the way for other cancer victims to get laetrile.

But it wasn't as easy as I thought to find a doctor who both would and could give the injections. Several of my medical friends went into high gear in the search, and while they were searching, I ordered some laetrile in the less effective tablet form.

Possibly Bill had taken one or two tablets when I looked at the calendar and saw that the appointment with the chemotherapist doctor was in two days. I phoned the G.P. and asked him to cancel it.

All this time the nurses had been telling me (as though I couldn't see it for myself) "Mr. Coakley is getting weaker." Then on Easter Sunday when Gerry came to bathe Bill while I went to Mass, she had shocking news for me when I returned. She told me she had discovered a lump below Bill's rib cage and toward his back.

Probably cancer riddled Bill's whole body! I couldn't pray except with the one-word cry, "Help!" I didn't want Bill to suffer any more, but to lose him would be like having the sun fall from the sky; Oh God, hold back the night.

The G.P. came the next day. Naturally, I told him about the new lump, and he examined Bill. Then amazingly he said, "Mr. Coakley seems better."

It didn't make sense. How could Bill be better when a new growth had developed? Bill was worse, but because the doctor thought Bill was better (or maybe because he *really* thought Bill was worse and so beyond help), he didn't mention chemotherapy. Anyway, I felt this was a miracle too— one with a new wrinkle. I decided it was the Blessed Mother's way of answering my plea, "Don't let them put Bill through the chemotherapy."

For a day or so I crushed the laetrile pills and put them in water or milk, hoping Bill could then take them, but soon his swallowing grew worse, and the graininess of the pills made him choke.

For the first time in his illness he was getting a mean bedsore because he had to lie on one side only; the latest tumor prevented his lying on his back or on his other side. When I talked to the G.P. by phone, he urged a nursing home, but if Bill had to die (and I began to fear that he did), I wanted him to die at home with me.

I did agree that he needed more nursing care. (He was less and less able to help himself move in bed, much less transfer from bed to wheelchair.) I engaged nurses to come in for five or six hours on different days. I had a week or so ahead booked, except for one day when a comparatively new-to-the-case nurse, Helen, was to come in for only two hours in the morning.

On that day, April twenty-sixth, Helen told me five minutes after she arrived, "Mr.Coakley looks worse than he did when I was here two days ago. I think you should have a nurse with you tonight. Do you mind if I phone the Nurses' Registry and try to get some one?"

I realized she was trying to tell me: Bill can die any time now, maybe tonight.

When her phone call came to nothing (nurses are often hard to get on short notice), she offered to stay "a bit longer."

"That's kind, but I thought you had a date for today and couldn't stay," I answered.

"I'll break it," she said.

I could only thank her. I knew that Bill was sinking drammatically before my eyes. In the two hours since Helen's arrival, his face had taken on a pinched look. I think I knew then that he was dying and for the first time I thought: DEAR LORD, I'M WILLING TO HAVE HIM DIE. HE'S SO MISERABLE. I DON'T WANT TO PROLONG HIS PAIN.

Perhaps it was a miracle that such a thought could come to me. Or Bill would have said it was just proof of his "Nudge Theory." He used to say that if the good Lord wanted you to do something that you balked at, He was ultra-patient. He didn't shove you forcibly toward it, but He did give you one gentle nudge after another so that bit by bit you yourself edged closer toward it, until finally, if you had any sense at all, you did it. Of course if you had had really good sense, you would have done it in the first place. Bill used as an example of his "Nudge Theory" a man who is drinking heavily and doesn't want to give up his precious liquor. Maybe he dents his fender when he's had a mite too much; that's Nudge #1. Then he messes up a business deal and gets in trouble with the boss; Nudge #2. Finally, with a few more nudges, like losing his job, or insulting his wife, he says, "OK, Lord, You've convinced me. I'll never take another drink, but You'd better help me stay off the stuff. I'm pretty darn weak."

Anyway, that day I thought for the first time: I'm willing to accept Bill's death, but, dear Lord, You'd better help me with the acceptance, and I repeated a prayer I had learned from Bill (though it certainly wasn't original with him.)

> Lord give me the serenity to accept the things I
>   cannot change
> The courage to change the things I can
> And the wisdom to know the difference.

Afterwards I wondered if Bill sensed my different attitude. Though he still fought fiercely for every breath, perhaps he no longer fought quite *as* hard as he had. Before the stroke he had always been a living antennae that picked up my moods. Sometimes I'd be disturbed about a contretemps of the day, and I'd think to myself: I won't bother Bill with such trivia when he comes home this evening. Then after he had actually gotten home, and we had been together a short time, he'd ask, "What's the matter, honey? Is something bothering you?"

Though I might at first deny it, I almost always ended up by telling him what was on my mind.

Whether or not he sensed my new attitude, I'll never know. I did know — I fully realized — that he was losing strength almost from minute to minute. The nurse and I tried to get the G.P. by phone and could not reach him. An answering service referred us to another doctor. This second doctor had never seen Bill, and I hated to call him now.

Helen said, "But we should have a doctor. Who does know Mr. Coakley? Who was that doctor who stopped by one day?"

She meant Frank. "Oh, that was a friend," I answered.

"Well . . ."

Although I felt that no human could do anything for Bill at this point, I agreed that it would be a comfort to have a doctor, and especially a doctor-friend as kind as Frank. I went to the phone and called him

It was now about noon, or possibly a little later. Frank arrived soon after my call. He said, "Bill has developed pulmonary edema and his type of stentorian breathing is . . ."

I interrupted to ask, "How long do you think he has?"

"Perhaps forty-eight hours," Frank answered, "but it could be a little more or a little less. He's still putting up a tremendous fight for every breath."

I was strangely calm. I asked next, "Then you think I should call the priest and Joe?"

Frank nodded.

Joe and Jeanne said they would take the first available plane from Nashville. Our pastor arrived only minutes after I phoned and went through the solemn ritual traditionally called "Extreme Unction." As I was thanking Father for coming and seeing him to the front door, Helen came downstairs and said to me, "Mr. Coakley is asking, 'Where is my wife?'"

Hastily I bid Father goodbye and raced upstairs.

Throughout his illness, from the day be began to talk in sentences, Bill nearly drove the nurses crazy with that one question, asking it, Gerry said, "literally every minute or two" whenever I was out of sight. The would-be reassuring remark, "Mrs. Coakley will be back soon," didn't stop him. He would reply, "You mean you don't know when the hell she'll be back. Where is she?"

He proved his prestroke dictum, "I always want you within patting-distance." In fact, even for the short interval that the nurses shaved or bathed him, and I wasn't in the bathroom with him, I could hear over and over again through the closed door, "Where is my wife?"

After he asked Helen that question, he spoke only twice more in the hours before he died. Once was after I had spoken to him first. Thinking to rouse him or to cheer him, I said in a light tone, "You know I love you, honey," and he answered, "I love you too."

I like to think those were his last words, but I am honestly not sure. At one point he did say, "Cigarette." (The prestroke Bill had been a heavy smoker, but for long after the stroke he couldn't smoke at all. After he developed cancer, Gerry would occasionally hand him a cigarette, and I figured: If it gives him any pleasure, well . . .) so I put a cigarette between his lips. I didn't bother to light it because I knew he couldn't draw on it. Incidentally, his lips were cracked and dry although Helen wet them every few minutes with ice she had wrapped in gauze. He became almost weirdly pale. I remember thinking: his skin actually looks whiter than the bedsheets. Then he was cold to the touch although he was perspiring. I learned what a "cold sweat" is.

Around five in the evening, Therese came by, expecting to make her usual run-in/run-out visit. Bill was not alert by this time, but he did seem to realize that another person had entered the room. His eyes turned toward her. Then, after she had been there only a few minutes, Helen remarked that Bill had lost consciousness and was in a sort of coma.

Frank had gone home some time earlier, so I phoned the G.P. again. This time I reached him and told him that Bill was much weaker and seemed to the nurse and me to be dying.

The doctor couldn't have realized the change in Bill; it had been so sudden, so precipitous. He answered, "I'm going out to dinner now, but I'll be back at eleven. Call me then."

But Therese who was there and could see Bill with her own two eyes did realize and, loyal friend that she is, she stayed on. She proposed, "You and Helen go down stairs and get some dinner. I'll sit with Bill."

As we were finishing our hastily-thrown-together meal, I had the impression that Bill called "Mary," although I didn't exactly hear him. I ran up stairs. Therese said, "No, he didn't call vocally, but," she added, "this is strange — very strange. I'm sure he called you in his heart, and you heard the call. Just seconds ago he seemed to come out of the coma. He opened his eyes and looked around as though he were looking for you, and then you came."

While she was speaking, I had reached for his hand and was holding it. For a second there seemed to be an answering grip, and then his hand went slack, and for the first time in our thirty-six years of life together, there was no answering grip. I definitely knew then, if I hadn't quite known before, that he was dying. His spirit already seemed far away, oriented not toward me, but toward Another.

Some time later— an hour?—two hours?— his breathing changed. It was no longer so loud nor so deep. Since the G.P. could not be reached until eleven, I phoned Frank.

Bill's breathing became shallower and shallower. I said to Helen, "I wonder if Joe and Jeanne will get here in time."

She said, "Maybe it would be better if they didn't."

I saw what she meant. I was glad that they had not been there when Bill was struggling for every breath. I had been preternaturally calm all day, but if I had been within the aura of their sympathy and love, I would never have held up.

The seconds ticked by. To facilitate Bill's breathing, Helen wound his bed up to the highest position so he was sitting as straight as an angle-iron. There was nothing else we could do. The three of us, Helen, Therese, and I, grouped around his bed motionless and silent as statues in a graveyard. There were a couple of times when I was sure he had breathed his last when he hadn't. He would seem to shudder and stop breathing, but then make one more immense effort and breathe again.

Helen said it was seven minutes past nine when he died. She lifted his hand, slipped off his gold wedding ring, and handed it to me.

⚜ Part Two

{14}

Finis. Bill's story is told, and so is my story as his wife.

By that story I wanted to reach my sisters-in-sorrow — all of you who are agonizingly bending over a sickbed — and show that the Lord is "a refuge . . . a helper in due time in tribulation."[1] Only by His grace could I have clung to the hope of a complete cure for so long, and only with that hope could I have lived through those four and a half years. Hope buoyed me up and, in a sense that most of the doctors could not understand, my hope was "realistic" because it supplied the "practical" help that kept me afloat.

Then I wanted to show that God hears prayers and, following His own timetable and His own formula, He answers them. Although He never gave us the full cure that I yearned for with such aching intensity, He did return to Bill faculties that every doctor on the case selfconfidently pontificated were gone, gone, gone. Lastly, as Therese said, He waited, oh so patiently and indulgently, to send the death summons until, on the morning of Bill's death, I found myself for the first time willing to have him die.

Now perhaps I should write a follow-up, a species of Book Two, telling my own story as a widow (and in lower case the story of other widows I've talked to) seeking to reach all of you who weep for a lost husband with the message that God shall still be "with thee . . . to deliver thee."[2] He will help you, brick by brick, to build up a new life.

If you had a satisfactory marriage, you feel that an earthquake has toppled everything in sight and that you are left standing in the heap of the rubble.

What can you do?

Well, you can't instantly start the rebuilding. You have to give yourself time to mourn, to grieve, to get your bearings. The experts speak of "working through your grief" and they declare that grief follows a pattern or has definite "stages."

Psychiatrist Elisabeth Kübler-Ross, M.D., lists for both the dying person and his family (the latter, she says, are usually a step behind the patient) denial, anger, bargaining, depression, and acceptance. Bernadine Kreis, free-lance writer and a widow herself, lists for the widow, shock, suffering, and slow recovery. Other authorities say the family of the deceased go through stages of rebellion, desolation, and acceptance.

It seems to me that I added a few more stages for good measure, though actually I could call some of them subheadings under the main ones of the experts. Then I suffered to some extent what Dr. Kübler-Ross called "anticipatory grief" while Bill was ill. Perhaps my "denial" took the form of begging a miracle.

Whatever I anticipated didn't spare me shock when Bill actually died. My list of stages would go something like this:

1. *Shock:*
   (a) A numbness and a feeling of unreality about everything including religious beliefs.
   (b) An emptiness, a void, and consequently an aimlessness, and a drifting, or a going-along with whatever comes up, or whatever somebody else suggests.
   (c) A craziness and a confusion, and possibly an over activity (alternated with withdrawal), and other efforts to run away from or to cover up reality.
   (d) Sporadic questions about why did it have to happen. Fears about what will happen next and other fears including a fear of living that edged toward the death wish.
2. *Realization:*
   Facing the fact that he is indeed dead and reacting to the fact with near despair and by bouts of self-pity and restlessness.
3. *Effort:*
   Trying to start a new life, or at least a new chapter of life by shouldering responsibilities, by setting to work in earnest, and by reaching out to others.

4. *Acceptance*:
   and, to one degree or another, contentment.

When you are going through all this, you usually aren't objective enough to know that you're passing from stage to stage. It's only in retrospect that you can say to yourself: That's not the way I was thinking a month ago or six months ago. Then progress toward acceptance is not upward in a straight line; it overlaps and often regresses, so it draws a line like that of a stock-market graph. The general trend over a year's period may be up, but in the interim the zigs and zags are plentiful. The only stages I'm sure come in the order I've listed are the first and the last.

Every widow I've talked to agrees that shock comes first. It certainly came first with me. One religious-minded widow-friend had this explanation which may have some validity. "The reason death is always a shock even if you're expecting it for a long time, is that in God's pristine plan, humans weren't meant to die. Death isn't natural, it's unnatural— it's something that warped our world when men turned from God with their original sin."

Be that as it may, after Bill died that night, I was so stunned that I was hardly aware of what was happening around me or, to the slight degree that I was aware, I had a strange, detached feeling as though it were happening to somebody else far off in a blurred Never-Never Land. Yet on one level I must have reacted normally to Frank's arriving, to Joe and Jeanne's arriving, to Therese's leaving, to Helen's leaving, and to the various phone calls people were making.

The only thing that made any conscious impression, however, was that everybody was trying to be kind to me. At one point, Jeanne led me back to the breakfast room, and I knew clearly that she was trying to spare me the trauma of seeing morticians carry Bill's body from the house. I sat there as though the matter were of small consequence. Maybe it was. Bill's soul was elsewhere. But I wasn't thinking of that; I wasn't thinking— period, except for one wild notion that came and went with the speed of sound: Maybe Bill isn't really dead; maybe he's just comatose; maybe I should run after those men and make them bring him back until we find out.

No doubt I was behaving in classic widow fashion. A widow-friend described herself as a "zombie." She said, "I made plans for the funeral, and I attended it, but I can't remember it."

Another widow said, "People told me I was 'wonderful' at the wake, so calm, so gracious, so affable. If I were, I didn't know it. I was off in outer space doing everything by reflex action."

Ruth Jean Loewinsohn in her book about widowhood spoke of functioning as though you were split in two. She said, "Part of you may be going through the motions of the funeral while another part of you watches and wonders how you can be so calm. It is normal to dissociate yourself from yourself . . ."

This numbness passes, but not for some days. It's nature's anesthesia that helps you function at a time when, if you were fully aware, you might go into hysterics or else collapse.

I remember only disjointed parts of Bill's funeral Mass. One sentence of the pastor's talk stands out. He said that when he gave Bill the last rites, Bill made the sign of the cross. It was a comforting thought that, although Bill couldn't talk, he could make this dying profession of faith. I remember too that the vocalist sang "Ave Maria" as I had requested, but I don't remember her singing my other request (one of Bill's favorites) "Thank God From Whom All Blessings Flow."

Afterwards I asked Father why my second selection was not sung, and he answered, "But Mary, it was! At Communion time."

I had not heard it. My mind was elsewhere. At Communion I remember telling myself: "I am united to God. Bill is with God. Therefore, I am also with Bill." But it was no more than a cold syllogism. I didn't feel Bill's nearness at all. I am not sure that I even believed it.

In fact, after Bill's death my faith seemed to fade away to nothingness. I wasn't sure of anything. Maybe this too was part of the shock. Years before I had written up a true story about a woman who had been separated forcibly from her husband when the Reds invaded Poland, and she never from that day on knew what had happened to him. I entitled the piece, "Where Is My Husband?" I certainly didn't think of the article in the first post-mortem week, but the words, "Where is my husband?" echoed and reechoed in my mind. They were to reecho even more frequently later. Right after the funeral I was distracted to an extent by having so many people with me. My wonderful family had rallied around. There was a contingent from Tennessee, Virginia, and New York. That included my grandchildren and Jeanne's widower father.

The actual burial I forget in *toto*. In my mind it was a blank space between the Mass and the time that a number of people came back to the house for a strange Alice in Wonderland party. (Joe and Jeanne, helped mightily by ultra-kind friends, had seen to the food, and friends and neighbors had sent in all sorts of casseroles, hams, cakes, and so on.) I half expected to see Bill circulating among the guests handing them fresh drinks he had made and saying half-jokingly, "It'll do you good and help you too."

I don't remember much of the next couple of days except that my family began to leave town one by one like the Ten Little Indians, and at the end of a week or so, only Katharine and Jeanne were still with me.

These two dear people helped me to attend to some business affairs and to address acknowledgements. I didn't like the usual engraved or printed acknowledgement cards with their stiff and stereotyped wording. I wanted to scrawl in my own handwriting at least the word "Thanks," and sign my name. Then I wanted the quotation from St. Thomas More, "Pray for me as I do for thee, until we meet merrily in Heaven" on the stationery. At a nephew's suggestion I had the stationery engraved. However, since my mind was so foggy, I made a mistake in the quotation; it should have been "that we may meet," not "until we meet," but I was glad of the mistake. "Until" gave assurance that I would meet Bill again when I died. I needed every little straw of assurance I could get.

After a while Jeanne left; she had to get back to the children and Joe. Then Katharine left. I was immensely grateful that they had been with me so long. I couldn't have managed without them, and I hated to see them go, yet— strange ambivalence— I didn't particularly want anybody to stay longer. They stayed just long enough, and no more. Way in the back of my mind I kept trying to come to grips with what had happened, and I couldn't do it. I now needed an empty house without the interruption of conversation to think things through and to think about Bill. I *had to* think about him. The need had become a kind of ravening hunger.

Also I wanted to mourn alone. In the final analysis, mourning is, and must be, a solitary business. Regardless of how much other people may have loved your husband and miss him, they cannot love and miss him in the unique way that you, his wife, do.

Alone-ness has the advantage too of privacy to cry. If you cry before others, they usually feel they have to say something comforting, and you feel you should dry your tears.

There is only one thing worse than crying, and that's not crying.

In fact, it probably helps if you scream aloud occasionally in the solitude of your own four walls. Maurice Lamn said in his book about Jewish death and mourning that Jews rend their garments and that "this rending is an opportunity for psychological relief. It allows the mourner to vent to his pent up . . . anguish . . ."

At any rate you have to grieve and you have to cry. The poet Charles L. O'Donnell was right when he wrote:

> Take no drug for sorrow; drain the cup
> Until you hold it bottom up.
> Know that pain's own bitter wine
> Is pain's only anodyne.[3]

Of course I didn't remember the poem in my early days of

widowhood, but I sensed that I had to "drain the cup," and in a strange way my grief, or at least my uninterrupted thinking about Bill, was my consolation.

Consolation? That's not quite the word, but I don't know what word to use. I did want to think of Bill, and yet my thoughts often brought only the feeling of a measureless vacuum, for Bill seemed utterly gone, and I was lost, bewildered, abstracted, and I no longer seemed to have religion to help me!

I certainly wasn't bitter about not receiving the miracle of a complete cure. In fact, I think that even then subconsciously I was grateful that I had been able, by the grace of God, to hold on to the hope of a cure for so long, and certainly I was grateful that Bill survived four and a half years after the CVA.

Nor was I dogmatic about disbelieving. I just couldn't reach out for the solid rock of faith; I didn't know where it was any more.

Well, theologians say that faith is not of the feelings, but of the will. Later, I tried to pray, "Lord, I want to believe. Lord, I will believe," but in the beginning I was too confused to do even that much.

Probably my faith remained in the depths of my soul, hidden by my murky emotions. In a happier time, religious truth had had sharp, bold outlines. Indeed, my first book written thirty years before (in effect, a spiritual book triggered by Bill's early-in-our-marriage conversion from agnosticism, or what he called "paganism" to Catholicism) contained, at the request of the editor, a chapter on death. I had written glibly then, sure of my beliefs. I spoke of a fictional Tom who had died, saying that "we can reach him and he can reach us" because we are united in and through Christ. "Although death shuts out his familiar face and touch, in many ways he is actually closer to us than when his arms encircled us."

And I went on, saying that on earth, "Always we wives and husbands are two distinct beings whose minds never completely merge, try as we might to break down all barriers by force of love and of passion. Oh, our thoughts and hearts often meet in exquisite sympathy and affection, only to separate again and we know 'He does not understand.' But in death he does understand— always. Our minds, our hearts, our souls are surely more open to him in the light of the eternal heights. We can pray for him (if he is still in Purgatory) and we can talk to him and ask his prayers for us whether he is in Purgatory or in Heaven, knowing that in God's embrace, we are united more closely than ever . . . This is the blessed wonder of the Communion of Saints."

Communion of Saints? That belief was a great comfort to me later, but in the weeks right after Bill died, I was not warmed or comforted by it. Like all other religious ideas, it had seemed to vanish.

Someone gave me a card with the message, "Death is only an horizon, and an horizon is nothing except the limit of our sight." Those words gave me no comfort either. My mind kept thrashing around, propounding questions. Was death really an horizon beyond which lay the glorious Promised Land? Or was death merely a cut off point like a backdrop of stage scenery, beyond which was nothing at all? In short was there an afterlife? I had always believed in one, but why had I believed? How did I know it was for real?

Was there any authority or documentation? Does the Church or the Bible say anything about it?

I honestly couldn't remember at first although every Sunday at Mass I heard in the Creed the words, "I believe in the resurrection of the body and life everlasting," and at Masses for the dead, Masses of *Resurrection*, the words, "Life is changed, not taken away."

And the Bible? All my life I had read bits of it here and there, and I had heard it read at Mass. Moreover, at the convent schools I had attended, my homework for Religion Class had often included memorizing verses from the Bible. Yet I couldn't think of a single biblical reference to immortality, and I wondered if any existed.

Just as though I were opening a tome as unfamiliar as the Koran, I opened the Bible and a concordance and began searching.

I found first of all the bald statement, "The dead rise again."[4] I found the long passage in St. Paul's epistle to the Thessalonians in which he said, "And we will not have you ignorant, . . . and grieving as do nonbelievers . . . who have no hope . . . the dead who are in Christ, shall rise . . . ."[5]

Altogether I found enough scriptural allusions to immortality to cover two typewritten pages.[6]

They helped me some, and months later a thought occurred to me that helped too: The very fact that death seems such an outrage is itself a proof of immortality. When you are very close to a person emotionally and he dies, you look at death with entirely new eyes and for the first time it looks unreal to you. You cannot accept it as genuine. Well, such nonacceptance would not be instinctive if the dead person were in fact life-less. Only his body is lifeless; his soul is life-ful.

Your husband is, Is, IS!

"An aim in life is the only fortune worth finding."
If Robert Louis Stevenson is right is saying that, and I think he is, you're doubly devastated.

First you've lost a person uniquely dear to you. (Oh, he may be alive spiritually, but he's not alive in the flesh.)

Second, you've apparently lost your vocation, your role.

I said to myself: Who needs me now? Not Joe. Not Jeanne. Not the grandchildren. I flatter myself that they love me, but they don't *need* me. Their lives are full.

You feel like the character who is shot in Act I. The play goes on, but you have nothing more to do on stage; you're just a useless hanger-on until curtain call. Or as I expressed it in my diary, "Without Bill, life seems just what Shakespeare's character called it, 'a tale told by an idiot, full of sound and fury, signifying nothing.'"

I said to Marie (a widow too) "I'm staggering around in circles."

She answered, "You'll stagger for a while, but some day you'll get your balance and your sense of direction."

She was right of course, but you can't or don't really believe it at first. I have my diary's evidence of how I felt. I wrote there, "Nobody can take Bill's place, that's for sure. All my family and friends, no matter how great they are, fail in one big way: they are not Bill.

"Knowing how miserable he was toward the end, I suppose I don't wish him back to earth to suffer more. But I can't think of his release. I can think only of my loss."

All grief, it seems, is essentially selfish. You don't really grieve for the dead person. You grieve for yourself.

Condolence letters are full of would-be comforting words, and some of them really do help *if* you can take them in.

"I know it's a comfort to you that Bill died at home," said one letter I received.

Yes, it was a comfort. Altogether, Bill was in the hospital eight times during his illness. If the doctor had come that final day, I'm sure he would have called an ambulance and whisked Bill away. The Blessed Mother gave me this last little favor of keeping Bill with me.

Another letter asked, "Do you know what feast day Bill died on? It's the day that the Church honors the Blessed Mother under her title, Our Lady of Good Counsel."

I hadn't known, and it was a comfort to find out. It was as though the Blessed Mother had sent me a little message, reading "I'll go on taking care of Bill even in death."

Several letters mentioned Bill's remarkable recovery up to a certain point, and I took great comfort in the fact that the "miracles" had kept Bill with me so long after the stroke.

One of my friends didn't understand this and she said, "It was harder on you that Bill died by inches. You had such a long drawn-out ordeal."

She was wrong about it being harder. Those four and a half years, though tragic, were in some ways the best years of my life. The stress of them proved to be the most fertile soil imaginable for love. My love for Bill grew and grew so I think *I* grew and became a better person. I remember leaning over his bed and yearning that I might, with a kiss, breathe new life and health into him. I truly wanted to share with him whatever I had of vitality and strength. I wanted to give him of my very self, of my very life. I never felt that intensity of love when Bill was well.

Paraphrasing the poet Coleridge's words ("He prayeth best who loveth best") I'd say, "He liveth best who loveth best." Not that I was so presumptuous as to say that I loved "best," but I did love better with each passing day.

To say "I love you" on any level is to boast because love always demands unselfishness. Once when Bill and I were talking about love, Bill said, "Forget the wordy definitions. You can define love in one word— giving."

But the more you give, the more you have to give and the richer with love you feel. That God gave me the opportunity to give and thus to enlarge my wealth of love was a tremendous grace. If I were to die tomorrow, I'd feel that I had lived because I have loved, and I am immeasurably grateful for that gift.

Despite all this, I didn't quickly come up with a Pollyanna cheerfulness. In fact, I wrote bitterly in my diary, "Widow! That's a negative word, meaning woman without husband, right glove without left, needle without thread, hammer without nail. Useless things, leftovers, discards— that's what widows and widowers are. The Hindus may have had the right idea with suttee, the custom whereby widows throw themselves onto the funeral pyres of their dead husbands.

My pastor said, "For the very reason that you had a good marriage, your sorrow is great."

That's true enough. Grief is in proportion to former happiness. You never want a good thing to end, and the better it is, obviously the less you want to give it up. Although I didn't wish Bill back, I didn't want to live without him either. I asked myself: What can I do between now and the grave?

One day I had an extended lunch with a friend, and when we said goodbye, she declared, "This killed the day for you."

Her words shocked me. I didn't want to "kill" a day. To kill time is only a little short of criminal. Time is life. I wanted to *use* it, and my problem was that I didn't know how. I overheard two of my friends saying, "The real miracle will be if Mary doesn't fall apart now. She's been so obsessed with the care of Bill all this time, and now she suddenly has no job."

What could I, what can you, do to stop "falling apart?" One of my widow-friends spoke of taking up "meaningful work." Although "meaningful" is a word that happens to irk me, her idea is sound. But what is meaningful?

I had to answer that question. You have to answer that question. And it's a poser. I knew that I would get back to my writing (after all, printer's ink is a habit-forming drug) but I wrote in my diary, "Will whatever I write be 'meaningful' now that Bill is dead? Will I, since my personal life is empty, have anything to say that I think is worth the paper its printed on?

"Oh, I might be fooled into thinking momentarily that it was downright important if it made me some money and won me some kudos. But I'd soon realize that it really wouldn't *be* meaningful unless it said something worth saying. Writing is based on what happens in a writer's mind and heart and soul. Before I can write meaningfully, I must lead a meaningful personal life. Or am I being pompous? I honestly don't know.

"Some people might say that to lead a meaningful life you should produce something useful, or acquire knowledge, or do 'good works.' But to that, I want to say, 'Nuts!' Rather St. Paul was right when he declared, 'And if I should distribute all my goods to feed the poor, and if I should deliver my body to be burned, and have not charity . . . I am become as sounding brass, or a tinkling cymbal.'[1]

"Maybe life can have meaning for me only if I still express love for Bill. How to do that?

"I can't tangibly, that's for sure."

I ended the diary entry on that pessimistic note, but it was only a day or so later that I had a thought that helped me. I believed that I could pray for his soul which might still be in Purgatory. The Douai version of the Bible says, "It is therefore a holy and wholesome thought to pray for the dead, that they may be loosed from sins."[2]

And it seemed to me that I myself, as a widow, was suffering a Purgatory-like pain for surely a great part of the pain of Purgatory must be waiting and waiting for full union with God in Heaven. I'm waiting, too, for the day I can join Bill and with him be united to God. I decided I could make my life an actual Purgatory for him just by offering up the waiting, the longing, and the loneliness as prayer for his soul.

Archbishop Fulton Sheen wrote that pain suffered without dedication was like an unsigned check — worthless. But once it is linked to Christ's suffering and offered to Him for a purpose, it takes on immense value. Therefore, prayer, which is always available, is the most constructive work possible.

To me, that was a heartening thought. I was also heartened and helped by several other thoughts, ideas, and suggestions that I collected as a housewife collects balls of string in a box, not always because I could use them immediately, but because they might prove useful later. My collection went into my diary.

First, a widow-friend told me, "Don't wrestle, nestle— nestle in the arms of God." She meant, I took it, don't fret and worry about what you should do with your life. Just stay close to your Father, and He will show you how to live.

Her advice was, in effect, a variation of Cardinal Mercier's "secret," which I also put into my diary. He wrote, "Every day for five minutes . . . close your eyes to the things of the sense world and your ears to all the noises of the world . . . . Then, in the sanctity of your baptized soul (which is the temple of the Holy Spirit) speak to that Divine Spirit, saying to Him: 'Oh, Holy Spirit . . . I adore You. Enlighten me, guide me, strengthen me, console me. Tell me what I should do . . . give me Your orders. I promise to submit myself to all that You desire of me, and to accept all You permit to happen to me. Let me only know Your will.'

"If you do this, your life will flow along happily, serenely and full of consolation, even in the midst of trials."

A nun gave me similar advice (another item for the diary) when she said that I should repeat Mary's words, "Behold the handmaid of the Lord,"[3] and ask God to use me. She assured me, "God will call you— give you work that is truly a vocation."

I tried to follow her advice, and the thought occurred to me that Mary, after Christ's Ascension into Heaven, was left alone. Literally the Light of the World had gone out. Yet she had to go on living— and certainly fruitfully. The Church should add to her titles that of Our Lady of the Bereaved. Addressing her by that title, I asked her to make me useful.

And I commented in my diary, "I suppose all through Bill's

illness I tried to use God as a means of getting something for Bill and myself, but now I'm asking to be used by God. I've been thinking that nobody needs me, but if God uses me, *He* needs me in the sense of Cardinal Newman's words. It might help to learn those words by heart. Anyway I'll type them out here in my diary:

> God has created me to do Him some definite service;
> He has committed some work to me which he hasn't committed to another.
> I have my mission ... I am a link in a chain, a bond of connection between persons.
> God has not created me for naught.
> I shall try to do good, I shall do His work.
> I shall be an angel of peace, a preacher of truth in my own place while not intending it — if I do but keep His commandments.
> Therefore I will trust Him,
> whatever, wherever I am, I can never be thrown away.
> If I am in sickness, my sickness may serve Him . . . .
> He does nothing in vain. He knows what He is about.

That was the last entry I made in my journal for some weeks.

{16}

Because in the beginning the reorganizing of your life seems so formidable and because (whether you realize it or not) you are not quite sane for a while, you usually don't have a clear plan for the future. You usually go along doing the things at hand and the things that are demanded of widows. First you have the job of tying up loose ends from your former life. Business affairs claim some time. So does the answering of condolence letters which keep coming in weeks after the funeral. As for the time that is left? Well, for myself, I didn't know what I wanted to do with it, so I filled it with whatever other people suggested to me. One of the suggestions or happenstances was the classic one for widows, travel.

Surely, there is reason for it to be classic because it does distract you with new scenes. You may not particularly feel like making the effort to go anywhere, but afterwards, if you do bestir yourself, you're usually glad.

In June, at Jeanne and Joe's suggestion, I flew to Nashville and then drove with them and the "Littlers" to Florida. The trip definitely did lift my spirits, despite the fact that on the driving part I had pain so acute that even today I wince thinking about it. Generous Jeanne had insisted that I sit in the front seat with Joe while she and the children sat in the back. We had driven into the mountains of east Tennessee when a thought hit me with the force of a physical blow: This is like the many, many automobile trips I've taken with Bill. Then a fierce tidal wave of longing for him suddenly came over me, and I felt as though I were drowning in grief.

Grief, I have since learned, comes in waves. It ebbs and flows, often catching you off guard. Sometimes, but not always, there is an obvious reason for its onset; you may open a book and see a scrap of paper with "his" handwriting on it, or you may open a drawer and see cuff links or a tie clip that he often wore, and you're taken from smiling to crying with a surge that you can no more stand up against than you could against a ten-foot wall of water.

That's what happened to me on the drive to Florida. Frantically, I thought: I mustn't let Jeanne and Joe see me crying and acting as though I'm not in a gala mood after they've been sweet enough to include me in this trip. I tried to choke back the sobs until my throat ached so agonizingly that I thought it would burst. Still I couldn't quite keep back the tears. They spilled over. I turned to the window and tried furtively to wipe them away as they welled up. Then, instead of blowing my nose all the time, I tried at least some of the time to sniffle noiselessly.

All this would have been bad enough, but then came the *coup de grâce*: Joe reached over and patted my hand. He couldn't have done anything on earth right then that would have been so comforting, but at the same time so devastating. On long automobile trips, Bill used to do exactly the same thing time after time. Some years before I had greeted one of these tiny displays of affection with, "Patting privileges belong to the driver," which for some reason amused and pleased him, and thereafter as he patted me, he'd say, "Driver's privilege."

Finally, we stopped for the night at some place in Georgia. I thought: Thank heaven, I can go into my room, shut the door, and at last cry freely. What a relief that will be!

When I got inside, I saw a duplicate of many rooms that Bill and I had stopped at in motels of the same chain. The furniture and the entire set-up was identical. Although it may have been a relief to cry freely, I could visualize Bill within that room more clearly than ever.

"But he isn't here!" Those words came from my heart if not from my lips as I looked around.

Once we arrived at the shore, I relaxed and felt some peace. It was only on returning home to Pennsylvania and arriving at the Philadelphia airport that I had another emotional upheaval.

During Bill's life time I had (when he couldn't leave work to go with me) travelled alone fairly often to see my family and occasionally to gather material for some writing assignment, but he always, without fail, met me at the airport when I returned. I don't know whether or not to say that Bill was a punctual person. Sometimes when I drove him to the suburban railroad station in the mornings to catch a train to town, he barely made the 7:55, and I can see him now running for it and swinging up onto the step after the train was in motion, all the while grinning back at me as though to say, "I didn't let this one get away." But whenever he had to meet someone, or particularly when he had to meet me, he was there before me, and whenever he met me at the airport, he should have brought along a folding cot and packed a brown bag lunch, he came so early. He said, "You can never tell when you might be caught in a traffic jam, so I'd rather be ahead of time. If I have to wait, I can always buy a paperback at the newsstand and read."

I even remember answering him once, in a very light tone to be sure, "If the day ever comes when I walk off a plane in the Philadelphia airport and you're not there, I'll never think of a mere traffic jam. I'll think of nothing less than death and desolation."

I thought of those words as I returned from Florida. What a stupid, featherbrained way to have spoken— as though death were a feeble joke. Now he was indeed dead. There was no grinning Bill with a book under his arm, eagerly striding to meet me. There was no Bill to collect my luggage and carry it to the car. Worst of all, there was no Bill to give me a welcoming kiss and a bear hug.

(It never occurred to me that when I went South during his illness, he hadn't met me and that hadn't bothered me. His being alive then made all the difference.)

As I boarded a bus headed for my suburban area, I was sure that everybody was staring at me. I felt conspicuous as though I were a sandwich man wearing cardboard signs proclaiming: My husband isn't here to meet me.

Then, after the bus reached its destination and I was waiting for a cab to take me the last lap of the journey home, I fell into conversation with a fellow-traveler and illogically felt that I owed her an explanation for my husbandlessness. Maybe, too, subconsciously I wanted to vindicate Bill's honor and prove that he wasn't neglectful of me. I don't remember what crazy thoughts scurried around in my mind. All I know is that they forced me to mention Bill to this complete stranger. I couldn't blurt out the harsh words, "He's dead." That would have been too painful. Besides, I had a strange feeling that, by those words, I would be admitting something shameful as though the widow-state carried with it a grisly stigma. Finally, I compromised by murmuring, "My husband is ill."

When she answered "Is he home now?" I was nonplussed and, because I didn't know what else to do, I nodded dumbly, telling a silent and a second lie.

One of the first books I read after returning from Florida was about bereavement. It contained this quotation: "From the moment a goose realizes that the partner is missing, it loses all courage and flees from the youngest and weakest geese. As its condition quickly becomes known to all the members of the colony, the goose rapidly sinks to the lowest step in the ranking order."[1]

The widow-writer commented that recently bereaved people felt the same — inadequate, apologetic, almost humiliated, and demeaned.

I couldn't identify with everything she said throughout the book, but *en route* from the airport I could have identified with the goose-quotation, and with the writer's comments.

(And one widow said to me, "Even if your marriage has been a stormy one, you have the same feeling because, whether your husband loved you or not, you were still an important person to him. As long as you're important to anybody, you know you are somebody. After you're widowed, suddenly you're not so sure. You have to wait for selfconfidence to return.")

When I reached home, I experienced another queer quirk. I dreaded entering the empty house. Although it was June, I felt a rush of chill air as I opened the door. I shivered. Then an eerie feeling came over me, and I thought: Maybe Bill isn't dead; maybe he's upstairs lying in his hospital bed waiting for me. Do I hear him calling me now?

That night I slept fitfully. I woke up several times, sure that Bill had called. Once I thought I heard a sound downstairs. Throughout Bill's illness, despite his physical helplessness, I had never thought of any danger. Now, with him gone, I thought of intruders and thieves, and I strained every nerve to hear the least sound.

Another widow told me, "I was worse than that, and not just when I got back from a trip. Every night for weeks I locked myself in my bedroom and put a chair beneath the door knob too. In fact, I was in such utter terror that I was afraid even to open the window."

So when I say that in the beginning you're not quite sane, I'm not exaggerating. The madness takes different forms with different people.

A sign of imbalance on my part was seeing men on every street corner who, in some way, reminded me of Bill. Once I saw a man striding up the church aisle ahead of me with broad shoulders and thick, wavy, grayish hair like Bill had, and I had an insane feeling that it had to *be* Bill so I hurried after him. I wasn't content with entering a pew behind him; I had to enter one in front of him so that I could turn around and look at him to determine if he were really Bill. (It wasn't until hours later that it occurred to me that Bill certainly couldn't stride for years before he died.)

Then small incidents that should have caused hardly a ripple affected me like an earthquake. There was the business of giving away Bill's clothes. It didn't bother me at all to phone two of his friends who were about his size and suggest that they stop by to see if there were anything they would want. As the first man was selecting suits, I smiled and very sincerely said, "I'm so happy you can use them."

Later, the second man came and took as many things, and I was urging him to take more if he wanted to, when he picked up a scarf that I had once given Bill and which was his favorite. When I looked at that familiar scarf that I had seen around Bill's neck so often, I felt a definite physical pain in the area of my heart, and I wanted to snatch it from the man's hand and cry: Oh no! Not that!

I had given away a whole wardrobe of clothes in excellent condition, but that threadbare scarf had me inwardly hysterical. My face must have shown how I felt, for the man put the scarf down.

Then another sort of inversion of values struck me over-hard. Why should mere things outlast people? Why should any*thing*, monetarily valuable or not, outlast an invaluable person? (Of course things do not outlast the soul of the person, but I wasn't thinking of that.) My mind spun in circles.

My mind surely spun again on the day I came across a typed speech that Bill had once given about insurance claims. (Bill worked in the home office of a large insurance firm as supervisor for the claims departments of its western branch offices in such places as San Francisco, Los Angeles, Denver, San Diego, Phoenix, and so on.) It opened with a Mark Twain joke that I had heard him tell in the past. Although I had never heard a second joke further along in the speech, it bore Bill's stamp; it was his brand of humor.

In fact, the whole speech was as individual as fingerprints. Reading it was like hearing him speak. He took a dull subject and enlivened it. Instead of just citing figures of property loss and disability compensation payments, he also described, in dramatic fashion, a fire in an airplane factory that caused the losses and the disabilities. By the time I finished reading the speech, I had gone into a veritable "fit" of crying.

But speaking of over-reacting, I can't omit my first visit to the cemetery. For a while I avoided the place, but came the day when I thought I should go to see if the stone I had ordered had been erected. I walked through the section where Bill was buried, and I couldn't find his grave. I wasn't really upset about

139

that because after all a grave holds only a body. Finally I gave up the search and headed back toward my parked car.

Then I happened to glance to one side and I heard myself cry out, "My God! My God!" So close that I could touch it was the stone engraved, WILLIAM DRUMMOND COAKLEY. I began to shake as though I had palsy, and my teeth chattered as though the temperature had hit zero. I don't think I was feeling sorrowful; I was just thrown into utter confusion. Certainly this violent upset was all out of proportion to the thing that triggered it.

Happily (because travel does help you regain balance and objectivity) another trip for me was in the planning stage that first summer. In August, my sister Katharine, her daughter and son-in-law were going to Europe, and they asked me to go with them.

The price tag made me hesitate briefly. (I wasn't sure with my new tax setup, just how much money I had to live on.) But then suddenly I *knew* that Bill had pulled some celestial strings and had arranged the whole thing. He wanted me to go.

Shortly before his stroke, the Wyncote Players' officers (he among them) had discussed the possibility of arranging a trip to England for interested group members. Bill and I were enthusiastic. We fantasized about taking side trips from London to Oxford, Cambridge, Canterbury, Stonehenge, Glastonbury, Bath, and so on. Then that trip fell through, and we said to each other, "Our next vacation will be in England."

Now, since he could not go himself, I felt that Bill had somehow leaned down from Heaven and whispered to my relatives, "Why don't you ask my favorite wife to join you?"

I enjoyed the trip though again I realized that you cannot leave your grief at home as you do your furniture. It travels with you— in the background for the most part but occasionally pushing to the fore. I remember one particularly poignant moment after we had gone from England to France and were visiting Chartres. As we entered the magnificent cathedral with its gorgeous blue and rose stained glass windows, the organ began to play, spilling forth rich, solemn, full-bodied sound, and I felt as though I were stabbed with the thought: Bill should be here! He didn't just *like* music; he had a passion for it and hearing it in that stupendous setting would have meant to him utter bliss. He used to say, "I get hungry for music as I do for bread."

But the poignant moments of this trip were far fewer than those of the first trip largely because it was planned and arranged in a way very different from Bill-shared trips of old. Then, too, I found that the *first* time you, as a widow, do anything alone that used to be a joint venture, is the hardest because it means breaking ground. Finally, time, each tiny segment of it, does indeed bring some healing. You may never get over wanting to share beautiful experiences with your husband, but, since you cannot, you stop brooding over it.

That's something.

17

"Time heals."

Well, cliché or not, that idea which ended the last chapter, holds much truth though it doesn't work according to Emile Coué, "Day by day, in every way, I'm getting better and better." As I said earlier, the progress for a widow has its zigs and zags. After my return from Europe then, and after my family left for the South, I retreated rather than advanced. I was more keenly aware of my alone-ness.

What could I do about it?

Even if I went to live with a relative or friend (and that was the furthest thing from my mind or anybody else's), I'd be alone in the sense that I wouldn't be half of a working partnership. And I didn't plan any other change either. My house, I decided, was as much home as any place was likely to be because it still held some warmth of "our" home, a place brimming with our marriage-memories.

A friend said, "You're not going to stay in that eight room house alone. You'll sell it." And I knew instantly I was indeed going to stay.

I was one of those widows who want to keep the home, precisely because I could look around and think: Bill hung that picture (saying, "Hey, Princess Eagle-Eye, did I get it right in the center?"); Bill used to polish those brass andirons (saying "Damn good job, eh?"); Bill planted those rose bushes, (saying "I cherish my wife with roses and wine.") To move to an apartment means "You can't take it with you"— not everything, and I was loath to get rid of any Bill-connected item.

To stay in the house, I think, was sensible in my case, but in no case should you make drastic changes of any kind (unless economics force you to) for at least a year. The postmortem shock lasts longer than you realize. Eventually, you will know whether you really want to stay or move.

In very early widowhood you may think you can't bear the painful sight of surroundings that remind you of your husband. One solution might be (if you can afford it, and if you have no nine-to-five job) to get out of the house for a while by travelling or by making a fairly extended visit to married children or other close relatives.

The same hold-off policy applies to getting rid of possessions. "You may feel that you want to get rid of keepsakes and mementos, but these very things may prove a consolation later. Rather than sell them or give them away, you can store them." I wrote those last words in one of my books before I was a widow, and (far more wisely than I realized at the time) I also wrote, "Many a widow has quickly sold her house saying, 'What do I want with this big place now?' only to find herself unhappy in an apartment where she has no garden . . . Many a widow has impetuously disposed of furniture as well as the house and moved in with the 'children' only to find her position as a resident mother-in-law far from comfortable. Many a widow has moved to a distant city to be near a son or a daughter only to miss, in the unfamiliar milieu, friends and associates of long standing who would give her the social life her children cannot provide."

Nor can you in every case move in with a much-loved sister, expecting everything to be the same as it was when the two of you were girls in the parental home. People change subtly with the years, and they change because they are influenced by the people they are close to. I know I'm a different person for having lived with Bill, and he became a different person for having lived with me. That's what a good marriage is: two people growing close and in some ways more alike with each passing year. Helen Keller put it beautifully when she said, "All that we love deeply becomes a part of us."

When I said something like this to one widow, she protested,

"You sound as though you're saying: Cling to the past. Surely that's morbid."

"No, I'm not really saying that at all," I answered. "I believe, as you do, that you have to look ahead because life is an express train that keeps moving and if you don't hop on you'll be left behind. But while you're on the train, don't obliterate the past and tell yourself it wasn't there. The past is part of the whole of your life, and you'd be less a person if you couldn't see it in the background."

Of course, with time and distance, it does recede naturally. I remember one day some weeks after Bill died pulling myself up sharp and realizing: I haven't thought of Bill all morning. That was really normal, but I was shocked. I felt guilty as though I had forsaken him and somehow proved myself disloyal. I was frightened, too, and I asked myself: What if I should forget him? That seemed the greatest of all possible calamities! It would be like having him die a second death, a death more final than the first.

That hasn't happened, and I don't think it can. My memories are a treasure trove. They give me, as Sir James Barrie said, "Roses in December."

A man whom Bill had once helped wrote in his condolence letter, "God was good to give me such a friend as Bill. I'll always remember him."

I'll always remember him, too, of course, though I don't behave quite as I did at first. In the early widowhood days, I felt like Madame Tolstoi; when asked if she often thought of her then-deceased husband, she replied, "I never think of anything else."

And such overblown thoughts as I had! Although before widowhood, I had always considered it rather ridiculous that some women practically canonized their husbands only *after* the poor fellows had died, I found that after Bill died, I was doing the same thing.

In fact, in talking to other widows, I've discovered that's almost standard operating procedure. A book I read recently about widowhood discussed this quirk and prescribed a remedy: Take a sheet of paper, draw a line down the middle, and on one side list a few traits that you particularly liked about your husband, on the other list an equal number that you disliked. Keep this paper handy so that when you're tempted to deliver a eulogy you can refer to it and see instantly that for every good point, there was a bad.

I can't quite endorse this gimmick because surely in most satisfactory marriages the husband's good points much outnumber his bad ones, but I did try to remember the words of a widow-friend who said, "When I find myself putting a halo on my Gus, I tell myself, 'Damn it! He wasn't perfect.'"

Why do widows do the canonizing bit?

Several of us widows discussed that question one day in my living room. The first to give an opinion said, "While my Al was alive, I didn't often tell him what a great guy he was. I guess I was half afraid he'd get a swelled head, or even fall from grace, if I did. I'm sorry I was so close-mouthed so now perhaps I instinctively make up for it by telling everybody else how great he was."

Although I laughed at her remarks, I'm inclined to agree that the canonization is, or can be, a sort of compensation, and in some cases a way of getting rid of any latent guilt you might have about not being fully appreciative.

Another interesting theory came from another widow. She declared, "You may overlook some of your husband's good qualities while he's alive. The fuss and muss of everyday living clutters everything up, and you miss some things you should see. It's only after you're a widow that you see the whole man."

"I think you have something there," I answered her. "While Bill was alive, it was like seeing a half-finished jigsaw puzzle; now it's like seeing the pieces all joined to make a complete picture."

In that picture you probably see some rough and murky

spots, but see above all (if your marriage has been a good one) a lifetime of love and loyalty and steadfast devotion.

Sometimes you see this devotion down to the tiniest gestures that you took for granted, and you wish you had not been so casual about it all.

There is probably still another reason for the canonization. Once your husband dies, friends, trying to be consoling, remind you of his good points, and you see them for the first time through other eyes. Several people said, or wrote in condolence letters to me, "I've never known a husband so obviously in love with his wife as Bill was." I saw then more clearly than ever that Bill never lost a kind of youthful exuberance about me, and incidents that I hadn't thought of in ages converged and thronged into my mind at once. Years ago, a young widow we met said, "Seeing the way Bill's eyes light up whenever you come near makes me want to try marriage again." And a man we met at a party after we had been married over ten years asked, "Are you two honeymooners? Bill acts like the proud and pleased bridegroom."

When people make complimentary remarks about your husband, you're happy at the tribute paid him, so don't spoil it by regrets about your own inadequate response. It seems more sensible to tell yourself right off: As long as I made my husband happy, nothing else counts— and certainly not some insignificant slip. Or even if the slip is fairly large, something far beyond those discussed in my living room, you can see that regrets are time-wasters. What can you do about past behavior?

Forget it, seems the best answer to that question. After all, as one wag said, "Life provides no erasures."

So to sum up in one sentence: Avoid both canonization and regrets.

Now anything else?

One more suggestion might help: Be grateful for having had a good husband and a good marriage. While you're feeling grateful, (although unfortunately you can feel sorry for yourself since you no longer have the good husband and the good marriage), fortunately you cannot feel like a deprived person. You have had your share of the pie— and maybe more.

As I look back now, I think that when I began to feel grateful, I took the first major step in the long climb back from the deep pit of grief toward acceptance.

18

"Whenever anything happens to me good or bad . . . my first impulse is to find her and tell her. She has the wonderful capacity for being neither unduly alarmed or unkindly calm— a kind of fathomless sympathy and support."

Reading those words of Malcolm Muggeridge about his wife, I thought: What happily married person doesn't feel that need to communicate? And often you get even more than sympathy and support; you get a solution to your problems because talking them over with a person as concerned about you as is your husband gives you perspective. Often, too, he is able to offer good advice.

After Bill died, since I thought far less of his ill days than of his well ones, I ached to talk everything over with him— not only problems. As one widow said, "Just to read the headlines and to have nobody to turn to and say, 'Look what the President has done now!' or 'Did you see what the Governor is up to?' makes news of the outside world seem illusory."

Alone-ness, you decide, is unnatural and strange, yet sometimes you feel you would as soon remain in solitary confinement in your home and hole up with your grief as make a social effort. You feel it's not much fun to talk to Hetty, or Hester, or Hilda. Why bother to get dressed up to go out with any one of them?

But whoa! That's foolish thinking. Inertia is an enemy. Life is for sharing. You need *other* people's company, and you need to try to help with *their* problems and to accept their help with yours. So early on, I knew I had better resolve to go out every day. Actually, it's a good idea "to keep your friendships in repair"— friendships with all sorts of people, married and single, men and women. You need sociability even more than happy married people do; they have it at home.

What I didn't see clearly at first were the social adjustments that widowhood calls for. Many are molehills, but, because your widow's vision is distorted, you see them as mountains. I remember my first sortie to the home of a married friend, Bea B. It was an all-women party like many others I had gone to in daytime throughout my adult life. But this was in the evening, and I wasn't used to driving after dark. Once the sun set and Bill was home from work, he always (on my few solo outings at night) chauffeured me. Then after he became ill and couldn't drive, I never left him at night.

Now I told myself: I have to begin night-driving sometime, and this is the perfect initiation because I'm not going far and I won't be getting home late. That reasoning was my tranquilizer as I drove to Bea's. By coming-home time its effects had worn off. I don't know what Bill could have done any more than I could have if a hoodlum had risen up from the floor of the car and stuck a gun in my face. Still I was uneasy because Bill wasn't there, and, for the first time in my life, I obeyed all the insurance company admonitions: before I slid under the wheel I peered into the back of the car looking for an intruder, and before I started the motor, I checked to see that all four doors were locked.

Then I thought: In the old days Bill always wanted to take care of me. Now surely he can take care of me just as well as when he was here at my side. Probably he has already asked the Lord for my safe-passage home.

But anyway, I began to talk — to pray — to him. I said aloud, as though I were phoning him from Bea's, "OK, honey, I'm ready to go home."

That didn't make me feel his nearness, but it helped me feel a calmness.

Fear returned a couple of nights later when Therese asked me to a little get-together at her home. Although I knew few of her guests, they had, at her request, prayed for Bill during his illness, so I gladly accepted the invitation.

149

I said before, the first time you do a widow-style action is the hardest; after you've worn a rut, it's easier, and you wonder why you ever wanted to reach for the panic button. However, to go to Therese's, I had to drive farther than to Bea's, and, as things turned out, I headed home later; it was past midnight. That reversed the rule and made this second night driving harder than the first. Again I glanced around uneasily and quickly locked the car doors, and, before I had my key in the ignition, I was talking to Bill, telling him I was ready for him to drive home.

These tiny apprehensive moments are comparative pinpricks. A worse jab comes when, for the first time, you go out with a man. A business friend of Bill's, in an *in memoriam* gesture I suppose, asked me to dinner. I didn't know him well, but I thought it was kind of him and I accepted. He took me to his country club where I found to my horror there was some sort of social affair for the general membership going on, and an army of people were milling about. A quiet conversation over the dinner table was one thing; fun and festivity, crowds and capers, another.

My escort said, "I thought you might enjoy meeting some of the people here. There are a number of widows. He steered me across the room toward a group of three women as he spoke.

Although I had mentally begun to apply the word "widow" to myself, I found it a shock to have somebody else matter-of-factly pigeonhole me. Was I to lose my identity and be classified from then on as a "widow"? I felt like Hester Prynne must have when she was branded with the letter *A*. Maybe every one of those women were people whom I'd very much want to meet, but I didn't want to meet them just because they were widows. I wanted to continue to know and hobnob with people in every state of life — with whomever I found congenial. Nonetheless, as though I were affixing a Halloween false-face, I put on what I hoped was a polite smile and I made conversation with the ladies in the approved manner.

Presently our little group moved toward the bar, and once we had drinks in hand, my escort excused himself for a moment. I thought: Is he going to leave me with these women until a curfew sounds?

Just then another man, and another friend of Bill's who happened to be in the club, came toward me to say "Hello." Naturally, I introduced him to my new acquaintances, but soon the three widows were talking among themselves, and he and I were having an animated conversation about a businessman's luncheon group which he, as well as Bill, once belonged to. Since I was talking about Bill, for the first time that night I began to enjoy myself. Then the man said, "It's been nice seeing you again, but I'll have to run along now. Ethel [his wife] is waiting for me in the next room."

I smiled and said, "Of course. Give her my best. And I hope I'll see you both later on this evening."

That seemed normal, for similar situations had arisen when Bill and I had been at a club affair. But what wasn't normal was having no Bill gravitate toward me when a conversation with somebody else ended. I don't remember ever having felt stranded as I did at that moment.

A lump rose in my throat, but again I tried to get my smile in place as I turned toward "the three graces," the widows, to take up with them where I had left off. At that point, my escort returned, and we headed for the dining room.

There was soft music, gourmet food — and dull conversation. I can blame the last only on myself. I never felt so wooden in my life. I kept thinking: I'm with the wrong man. At the same time, I realized he was doing me a kindness by taking me out and that I should be as pleasant and sprightly as possible.

By this time though, I felt I was a mannequin; I felt my face was forever set in a hard smiling mold so that if I should try to change its expression, it would crack and shatter like glass. I tried to sneak furtive glances at my watch, all the time calculating how soon I could politely suggest leaving.

Then I found out there was to be staged entertainment. How long would this last? An hour? Two hours?

Finally, after ages it seemed rather than hours, we were on

our way home again, and I'm afraid I let an audible sigh of relief escape me.

At that, I didn't go as far as Isabella Taves. In her book about widowhood, which I read months later, she tells of her first dinner party as a widow, where an unattached man was earmarked her partner for the evening. Although she had willingly accepted the invitation, she found, once she arrived on the scene, that she couldn't take it. She said, "I broke down completely . . . [and] spent the evening in my hostess' bedroom sobbing to my embarrassment and everybody else's."

My first venture was definitely my big hurdle. I've gone out a *few* more times with other men and have had some pleasant evenings. On the whole though, since widows outnumber widowers, an oldish widow does not meet many men and those I've met had interests that I couldn't easily mix-'n-match with mine. A couple of men talked to me about their businesses but were inarticulate about many of the subjects that could have kept Bill and me talking for hours on end.

Then one man said, "I'm sure you feel as I do. My wife had suffered so much that now she's gone, all I feel is an immense relief."

Well, maybe that's an unselfish way to feel, but it wasn't at all the way I felt; I felt grief, not relief.

One night I gave a little dinner party and invited this man. He took over the drink making and in general acted as host and man-of-the-house. He was trying to be kind and helpful, but unreasonable me— I half-resented him and thought of him as a usurper. On the other hand, I'm sure if he had not been helpful, I would have resented that just as much. I would have thought: This ignoramus doesn't know how to behave.

So you have to acknowledge that some of your social difficulties are, as a widower said, "just in your head."

Now, before I drop this subject of socializing with men, I must remark one thing: It rather surprised me that there are any number of widowers who have entered the senior citizen age bracket, looking not for companionship or marriage, but for a bedmate. I happened to sit next to one such man on the plane coming home from Florida, and he spoke quite plainly of his goal.

But the hardest thing to accept is the fact that widowhood makes for a certain awkwardness with some married friends of long standing. Although my married friends have been (in Coleridge's phrase) as kind and comforting as a "sheltering tree," I felt, particularly in the beginning, I couldn't discuss with them at length what was uppermost in my mind, my grief. I might dissolve into tears and embarrass them, or they might not understand how I felt, or if they did understand to a degree, I still felt it would be bad taste to discuss in depth what they had not experienced and could not respond to in kind. Ergo: I held back the words I wanted to speak and instead prattled foolish froth.

They, for their part, skirted daintily around the subject of Bill, apparently believing that mention of him would make me feel badly. No doubt it would, but never mentioning him made me feel worse. I didn't want people to go on mourning Bill, but I did want assurance that they remembered him. This blue pencilling of the deceased's name is a comedy of errors. One widow described the situation when she said, "I began to think there was a pane of glass between me and the rest of the world, shutting me off so I couldn't communicate."

Then the first parties are an ordeal — even family parties. A widow-friend said, "When I went to a family baby shower, I was utterly miserable. Everybody was standing around in groups of twos and threes laughing and chatting about trivialities while I was carrying this crushing weight on my heart. I felt: I don't have anything in common even with my own family any more. I'm as much an outcast as a biblical leper."

This sort of feeling passes, and you appreciate the friends who keep invitations coming. A few friends that you and your husband used to see frequently don't invite you, a single, as often they used to invite you, a spouse. And sometimes at parties you are invited to, particularly the first ones, you are conscious of the fifth wheel syndrome. It's a fact of life: the extra woman is labelled Liability; the extra man Asset.

I remember vividly the first time a friend asked me to stop in for a drink. To make me feel comfortable about accepting, she added, "You won't have to face many people. It's just a small party."

Well, the fact that it *was* a small party made the fact that I was the only husband-less person there all the more evident, and I ended by feeling all the more "the odd woman." I inwardly echoed the plaint of the girl in Carson McCuller's play (The Member of the Wedding), "All other people can say 'we' . . . All people belong to a 'we' except me."

I should blush to think how absurd and super sensitive I was throughout that first solo-flight cocktail party. At one point, the hostess said to her husband, "Get Mary another drink," and I felt somehow that she was patronizing me, the "poor widow," who needed looking after.

I had an equally unreasonable attitude on the next social occasion. A friend had invited me to a family dinner. I enjoyed the evening, but when it came time to go, my hostess said to her husband, "See Mary to her car."

The words struck me as offensive. They made me feel as though I were a pitiable wallflower. I didn't want any man to see me to my car if he had to be asked to do it. Subconsciously I must have made a very unfair comparison: this man, a casual friend, versus Bill, my husband who had loved me dearly. Bill had always acted as though he were the lucky guy who had wangled a date with Miss America when he escorted me anywhere.

Of course my reaction was less than sane, but, nonetheless, my feelings were so intense that I drove home in tears.

In part, I think I was crying because the tiny manifestations of widowhood, none of them important *per se*, were constant reminders of my love-loss. I can't analyze myself with assurance at this late date. Another widow told me recently, "The hardest thing for me to take is the realization that nobody loves or cares about my wellbeing as much as my husband did."

Then, as a new widow, you feel that your *amour-propre* suffers because you are awkward in handling social situations you've never before encountered.

Another time when I was invited to dinner, I didn't have to go alone. Other guests (a couple who were good friends of mine too) offered to pick me up. Even here was a slight snag, or at least a perplexity. If Bill had been with me, I wouldn't have thought twice of the four of us carpooling it to the party. Alone, I felt a bit odd and thought: The next time, if there is a next time, it would hardly be according to Emily Post's dicta for me, a lone woman, to offer to pick them up. What'll I do? How does a widow function socially?

It took me a while to see that there are alternatives. I could take chauffeuring friends an occasional bottle of wine or do them other little favors.

Slowly you catch on. You realize the number and the nature of the changes to be made in your social life all along the line. For one thing (although I'll never want my friends to be exclusively widows), you often find yourself seeing more of women who are also husbandless. Until Bill died, I had (aside from Marie, whose husband Bill and I had known well) few close widow friends. After Bill died, a number of widowed acquaintances rallied around, and it seemed natural to hobnob with them. The first man to take me to dinner had been right in introducing me to widows; his mistake had been in doing it too early.

In some cases, other widows help more than psychiatrists and clergymen in straightening out your thinking. They blazed the path ahead and can direct you. In fact, a small group of us met fairly regularly. Not that we talked about our woes hours on end — Heaven forbid! — but through a few words here and there we learned something from one another.

Incidentally, speaking of clergymen, a very kind priest, trying to show sympathy toward me, once said he understood my loneliness and added, "I remember when my mother died. I'd sit in the rectory and every time the phone rang, I'd think: If only it were Mom calling."

But in my tetchy state his words irked me. I wanted to retort: A phone call! Is that all you miss? I'm used to sitting across the breakfast and dinner table every day with my husband. I'm used to spending warm companionable evenings with him. I'm used to sharing my bed with him. As C.S.Lewis said (in his book, *A Grief Observed*) the thing that he missed after his wife's death was the "the thing I can never get. The old life, the jokes, the drinks, the arguments, the love-making, the tiny, heartbreaking commonplace."

Lay people who have skipped marriage are, of course, far less understanding than are clerics. One morning after I had dreamed in a mixed-up way about Bill, I woke up sobbing. I wanted to talk it out with somebody to make sense of it all, and I thought with a certain disappointment: I have a lunch date with So-and-So; she's never been married; she won't understand.

Because my social life had taken a new twist and was less satisfactory than of old, I decided after some months that I should explore ways to meet with people on a basis that was not always strictly social. Since I had my writing (and I did manage to sell a few magazine articles even in the first year of widowhood), I didn't want a full-time, outside job. (For many widows, regardless of monetary need, obviously that kind of job is a great psychological help.)

Instead, I jumped into a veritable MARY-Go-Round, sometimes with two or three engagements a day. I joined a group of men and women who met a minimum of once a week (and who could, if they wanted to, meet a maximum of three times a week) to go to lectures on everything from philosophy to basket weaving, from business law to flower arrangements; I got a job teaching Creative Writing one night a week at the Adult School of the local high school; I enrolled in an Art Appreciation class at the same Adult School another night a week; I tutored a college student in English; I attended to my financial affairs; I still tried to reserve not less than two hours a day for writing; and I took part in a Wyncote Players' play.

The last I didn't exactly plan. A friend who was to direct the play phoned and asked if I would take a role. I hesitated. Though Bill had been in more plays than I, our Little Theatre activities had always been in tandem. If he had a part and I didn't, I usually worked on props or served as prompter so that we were together for most rehearsals, and, of course, we always went together to the cast party after the last performance.

But then my hesitation switched to assurance. I felt that Bill would have said, "Why not, honey? You'll enjoy it."

After I left the phone though, I wondered about going to rehearsals a couple of *nights* a week for six long weeks, and I almost regretted my quick decision. I murmured, "Bill you got me into this."

I needn't have worried about all that night driving. The next afternoon a widower-member came by the house. He said, "I hear you're to be in the next play. So am I. How about my coming by on rehearsal nights and picking you up?"

I smiled. Bill had thought of everything, even an escort.

All my activity I think helped in the second half of that first crazy year.[1] For one priceless thing, it enabled me to make a few new friends, and, as a widow you do need some new friends simply because you see less of your old friends and because, whether you like it or not, you are beginning a new chapter of your life. "The old order changeth . . . ."

However, by the mid-part of the second year I slowed down. I began to heed Lin Yutang's words about "the noble art of leaving [some] things undone." He explained, "The wisdom of life consists in eliminating nonessentials."

Incidentally, while I was running around frantically, the daughter of one of my friends said, "It's wonderful. You're really liberated now. You were a prisoner in your own house for so long nursing Mr. Coakley. Finally, you can do your thing."

"Ummm . . . yes," I murmured. I couldn't explain to that sophomoric girl that, although I was freer than I had ever been in my adult life (no son at home, and no husband either ill or well) and although writing and lectures and so on were indeed my thing, I felt anything but free; I felt frustrated. As long as Bill lived, I was doing what I wanted to do above all else; I was functioning, not only as Mary Lewis Coakley, but as Mrs. William Drummond Coakley. The comfort and the confidence of having two legs to stand on was my Supreme Thing, that thing that had brought me the greatest fulfillment. Now I felt crippled and hampered rather than liberated.

Another friend spoke of my "burden" being lifted, and again I didn't explain that a bereaved wife of a good marriage would gladly resume that "burden" for, in a sense, it was no burden. You feel like the boy in the old posters of Boys' Town USA; they showed him carrying a younger child and the caption read, "He ain't heavy. He's my brother."

To those who have carried such a "burden," no explanation is necessary. To those who haven't, perhaps no explanation is possible.

19

"There is no peace unto the wicked . . ."[1] — nor unto the widow. My list of stages shows more headaches to come. I haven't said anything yet about those buzzing mosquitos, the "Whys."

One widow said, "Here I am months after Allen died still asking myself: Why me? I know a lot of women who are divorced, or unhappily married, but it had to be happily-married me whose husband had the heart attack and died. Why?"

At that time, I had already been through the "why" stage. In fact, it had been most virulent, not when Bill died, but when he had the stroke, so I told her how I coped with it. I had been plagued with such questions as: Why should Bill have been hit with this devastating illness when he had the vigor and vitality of a man a third his age? Why didn't it hit someone who was sickly and feeble to begin with? Later I asked: Why did Bill die when so many unloved people in nursinghomes live on and on?

Though it took a little while, I did eventually see that it is just as logical to ask contrary "Whys." Why did Bill have so much vim and vigor for so long? Why did Bill live so many years instead of dying at a younger age?

Then, one day, standing in Bill's den and looking at his bookcases crammed with hundreds of books on the Civil War and at so many other histories, I thought: all those years of reading and thinking and storing knowledge, what good are they now? They are buried with Bill. Why didn't God take some ignoramus, or some moron? Why Bill?

Again the answer came rather promptly even if I didn't exactly like it. When God calls the intelligent and the stupid, the educated and the uneducated, the beautiful and the ugly, perhaps he is trying to tell us, the survivors, "Watch ye therefore, because you know not the day nor the hour."[2]

If only the useless, the wicked, the infirm, the incompetent, the insane, and the woefully ignorant were to die before reaching doddering old age, no one would think of death at all. Prideful human nature wouldn't let you admit that you fell into any of the undesirable categories, so you would think that death before age ninety impossible to you, a desirable.

When death came then, you might meet it even less prepared than you are likely to be under the present set up.

I told myself: Thinking about death as I have since Bill died may help me to be provident and "lay up . . . treasures in heaven . . . ."[3] As one wise man wrote, "There's a great future in store for those who think about eternity." And who was it that said, "Remember your last end and you shall never sin?"

Eventually, you stop the "Whys" because you realize they're absurd. If you could figure out the mind of God, you would be a sort of god yourself. The ways of a Supreme Being would have to be "unsearchable" to mere humans. When I had a bad case of the "Whys," I told myself: You're acting like a child who decides she'll walk to the horizon and touch the sky.

After you've routed the "Whys," you find there are other troublemakers to deal with. Especially the first year, there may be flash-fears about everything from finances to family matters. One widow said, "I was terrified and baffled about investing my insurance money."

To some extent that's a healthy fear because brokers often press widows to buy stock which they say has "tremendous growth possibilities," but which, in reality, is simply a stock they've been told by the firm to push. Getting a broker, a lawyer, and an accountant whom you are sure you can trust is a must. I stuck with men whom Bill and I had had for years and didn't listen to newcomers who used fast-talk about "investment opportunities."

"Beware" is a word to remember.

"Education" is another. You might do well to take a course in

160

investing and/or in money-management. The brokerage houses sometimes offer such courses gratis. The trouble is that the teacher, who is usually a broker, wants your business and tries to persuade you to give it to him and to buy the securities he's pushing. Although I had handled some investments all my adult life, I took such a course and was horrified to see the gulli-bility of one of the widow-students. The teacher talked about stock-options and the profits some people make. The student sat there wide-eyed and eager as a teenager with visions of a new sport car, and, as we left the hall later, she turned to the teacher with questions about investing in options herself.

She wasn't young, and I wanted to, but didn't, butt in and say, "What you should have above all at your age is safety and a good return on your money. Don't take risks. Options I consider speculative."

One inexperienced widow told me, "I'd never handled invest-ments of any kind, so I just turned my affairs over to my son."

Probably in her case that was wise. In another case where a son is very young and as inexperienced as you are, it might not be wise at all to hand him everything you possess, or even a sub-stantial part of it. Of course, if you have had some experience, you may just naturally continue the do-it-yourself route of years standing, and you already know the pitfalls.

Investments are not your sole financial concern. I often feel harassed and afraid I'll overlook some important details such as: paying the estimated state and federal income taxes, each due four times a year; paying the Pennsylvania Personal Property Tax; paying the real estate tax; clipping bond coupons prompt-ly; keeping all records that might furnish deductions for the April Federal Income Tax Report; keeping up my insurance policies by paying the premiums when due; having the car go through state inspection within the time-period prescribed by law, etc.etc.

To help squelch this type of fear, I keep a book-like calendar that I consult every day, and I keep a fair-sized filing cabinet with separate folders for insurance papers, income tax records,

161

credit card numbers, appliance guarantees and many other items.

Stock and bond certificates go in my safe-deposit box at the bank. I always staple the brokerage slip to them so that if the time comes when I want to sell, I have a ready record of the purchase date and price paid, which you must report for the Profit and Gains Tax on your income tax report. But I also keep a ledger at home where I write this information and more. I want the facts right at hand for easy referral.

Naturally, everybody keeps cancelled checks for a few years.

Despite this pesky record-keeping and bookkeeping, you may still have moments of fearing that all is not in order. I do. And I have to calm myself with the text about casting care upon the Lord.[4]

Then, what widow doesn't have fears for the formless future? You ask yourself: Where will I be next year? Five years from now? Ten years?

I tried to banish that *bête noir* by telling myself sternly: You didn't worry about that while Bill was alive, why worry now? And life comes not by years, but by days and hours. Face today, and in the morning face tomorrow. Live from day to day and leave the future to God. You can trust your Father.

Then there's a jumble of unreasoning, lesser fears. One night I woke up in the wee hours and looked out the window. It had snowed, and all the houses, trees, and bushes had lost their distinctive outlines under the heavy white pall. Nor was there a line between the road and the lawn; they ran together and seemed flattened out into one unbroken expanse of wasteland without a single footprint or a car-track.

Although you might say that the scene bespoke peace and serenity, it seemed strangely foreboding to me. I felt as though I were alone in an alien, uninhabited world; no living creature existed besides myself. For a moment terror gripped me like a hand at my throat. This terror wasn't like the fear of intruders or thieves that I had felt on that earlier occasion. I wasn't afraid of anybody or anything tangible. It was simply a baseless fear of being alone, starkly and totally alone.

Other widows have told me since that such baseless fear is not unusual, and even the tough old sea captain had his fears of solitude; he said, "I have never known a man brave enough to go into the woods alone at night and shout his own name three times."

Obviously, if you have reasonable fears of intruders— or if you don't have them, it's wise in these days of a high crime rate, to take what precautions you can against anybody breaking in. It has also helped me psychologically to remind myself: I am not really alone, "For though I should walk in the midst of the shadow of death . . . thou art with me."[5]

But I feared, too, since I lived alone that I could die in the house without anyone knowing and without anyone discovering my body for days on end. I saw myself falling down the cellar steps and breaking my back or my hip and lying there on the cold cement floor to die agonizingly and slowly because I was unable to get up and call for help. None of my friends would think there was anything wrong if I didn't answer the doorbell or the phone; after all, I went out every day. Even if they tried to get me several days in a row, they wouldn't think twice about it. I had always gone to Tennessee fairly often, so they'd conclude that I was southward bound again.

It didn't occur to me when I had these fears that I had given my doorkey to my nextdoor neighbors, Deana and Ray, so if they didn't see my car going in and out of the driveway, they'd probably check on me. Moreover, if they ever did check under these circumstances, they would find that I had written labels and attached one to the upstairs phone, the other to the downstairs phone, giving the numbers of Joe, the police, and the fire department.

And early in my widowhood I knew nothing of Contact. This organization described itself as "a twenty-four-hour-a-day, seven-days-a-week Christian telephone ministry open to all faiths and serving people gratis in seventy-six cities of the U.S." Although Contact serves people who are "lonely, troubled, depressed, or desperate," it also has a Reassurance Service, by which it provides someone to phone live-alones, at a prearranged time every day just to see if the person is OK. If the phoner gets no answer to several successive calls, he or she phones the person whom the live-alone has designated as an interested family member, friend, or neighbor.

As the wit said, "So many things we're afraid of never happen," or there is a way out. Besides, it occurred to me recently to ask myself: Why should I have worried about the physical circumstances of my death when I worry scarcely at all about its spiritual circumstances. Moreover, if I believe in prayer, and if I pray with any degree of sincerity, then I have a gilt-edged guarantee that I'll be taken care of somehow at death by the "Hail Mary." In it, I plead, "Pray for us sinners . . . at the hour of our death."

But perhaps my strangest fear was (and is), the one that comes any time of day or night: it was that I would live on and on into some distant future where Joe and Jeanne and all my family would long since be dead. Having outlived Bill, I somehow felt that I might outlive Joe. In fact, I felt I might live to be over a hundred like the fabled Hanzukuts of northern Pakistan.

I was surprised when I talked to another widow who mentioned the same fear. She had had two children, and one had died in his twenties. Now that her husband too was dead, she feared the death of her other child while she was still alive, and she said, "I'd rather die right now— today, than have that happen."

That night, feeling low myself, I thought: She's right. I'd rather die now too. I'm only marking time now.

But quick on the heels of that thought came rebuttal: Never in life do you just mark time. You are either moving forward or backward spiritually. This life should be preparation for another life, and the prep job from childhood to old age is the job of top priority.

My thoughts ran on, and I remembered that some months before Bill died I said to him one day, "If you get to Heaven before I do, reach down a hand and pull me up." Though I had, of course, been half joking, I felt almost disappointed at the end of the first widowed year that he hadn't pulled me up. Then one

164

night, saying the rosary, I came to the "mystery" of "The Finding of Jesus in the Temple," and I was trying to meditate on Mary's joy at reunion with her Son Whom she had lost for three long days. Instead, I found myself meditating on my joy at meeting Bill someday in Heaven. But I had to admit that if Bill were to pull me up right now, with my sin-begrimed soul, I couldn't go straight to Heaven. If I went as is, I'd feel as uncomfortable as the little girl who dreamed she was at the birthday party dressed in torn blue jeans when everybody else was in frilly white dresses. According to the teaching of my Church, I'd have to go to Purgatory first. This stopover would mean (since Bill was probably already in Heaven) a delay in our meeting.

Now, I reasoned, sin can be purged, not only in Purgatory; it can be, and should be, purged primarily on earth by prayer, penance, and good works, and the prayer I could offer God would be the prayer of suffering— suffering emptiness and loneliness.

Because earth's purgation is voluntary, it could work faster than the purgation of Purgatory. In other words, my prolonged living may hasten, rather than delay, our meeting. It's quite possible that Bill may win me the favor of joining him (and God) as soon as can be, given my sins. (Incidentally, I was, and am, inclined to put God in parenthesis as an afterthought to Bill, which some people might say verges on the blasphemous, but which, I fear, is characteristic of once-happily-married widows. Marie said, "If I longed to be with God in Heaven the way I long to be with my Paul, I'd be a saint.")

Another day when the death wish turned up like the bad penny, it brought with it other thoughts: You don't *really* want to die. Suppose you went into the U.S.mint and saw waist-high stacks of hundred-dollar bills and stacks of empty boxes. Then suppose a voice said, "Fill as many boxes as you'd like. You can have all the money you can pack up. Do you want ten minutes packing time or thirty?"

You'd answer, "Thirty minutes— or as long as I can get."

OK, the longer you live, the more opportunities you have to

win grace. You're losing opportunities now by mooning over your phoney death wish.

Yet even after this self-lecture, the "I'd rather be dead" thought has occasionally popped up again. One widow who said it has also assailed her, opined, "It's because we're romanticizing and dramatizing ourselves."

Touché! I know *I* romanticized about death. I often relived an unforgettable day when Bill and I, vacationing in California, stood together on a mountainside watching the sun set over the bay. It was one of the most spectacular sunsets I've ever seen in my life. Its beauty and splendor were overpowering. I wanted to fall to my knees, or shout, or sing, or cry, but actually I just stood there awestruck. The thought flashed across my mind then: This is a preview of eternity; Heaven will be like this. I'll be standing hand in hand with Bill marveling at the glory of God.

Then shortly after Bill died I read *Life after Life*. Its author, Dr. Raymond A. Moody Jr., speaks of the patients who were resuscitated and "brought back to life," after they had "died." He said they often described being welcomed in "the beyond" by some dear, predeceased relative.

I envisioned Bill coming to meet me as I moved heavenward. The scene was a rerun of the home-from-the-South scene that I described earlier in this book. Our exquisite joy was almost painful in its intensity. We clung to each other with a tenderness that was more poignant than passion. No wonder I sometimes wished I were up there now.

Did I really mean it however? Or was I kidding myself? Although I thought my occasional and fleeting death wish was genuine, I inconsistently held onto life. When I had a bad cold, I hoped it wouldn't turn into flu. Moreover, after Bill died, I was more conscious than I had ever been in my life of little aches and pains — so much so that I sometimes feared I was becoming a hypochondriac. As my sister Katharine said, "Everybody wants to die of perfect health."

The fears and the (bogus?) death wish are often a facet of the craziness.* Once I had a twenty-four-hour virus and I thought: I'm dying!

Shades of Sarah Bernhardt! Of course self pity was behind my posturing. Although it's not exactly jolly to feel weak and feverish and have nobody in the house who could bring you as much as a glass of orange juice or a slice of melba toast, it isn't fatal, and you know you should tell yourself: "Snap out of it. Self pity is destructive."

---

*Obviously, there are exceptions— a few cases when you should take your small ailments seriously. Some studies, including that of Colin Murray Parkes, and of the Montefiore Medical Center (Bronx, N.Y.) indicate that a bereaved woman is more likely to die or become gravely ill than a woman of the same age and circumstances who is happily married. And British psychiatrist Michael A. Simpson wrote interestingly enough, "A high proportion of the increased death rate after bereavement seems to be due to heart disease, especially coronary thrombosis (so the 'broken heart' is a very real phenomenon.)"

20

" **S**elf pity is destructive."
As I wrote those words at the end of the last chapter, I thought: Self pity is such a menace that it should have a chapter to itself. I found that it sneaks up on you, and you don't always recognize it for what it is; you confuse it with grief which it is not.

One day self pity even had me lamenting that I'd have to die without Bill at my side. I mused: I was with him when he died. I held his hand and surely that gave him some comfort. He won't be there to hold my hand.

Well, if I had to reach that far for something to feel sorry for myself about, it would seem that I have a pretty fine life. But, nonetheless, I was really succumbing to the "poor me" syndrome, and my common sense had to be called in to address the issue and point out: If you truly possessed the faith instead of merely professed it, you'd remember that Bill is close to you in spirit. Ergo: he *will* be with you when you die. What's more, Bill, now united to God, can help you face death better than you, in the flesh, helped him.

That particular self pitying thought fled, but, as one widow said, "Getting ride of one reason for self pity is like cutting off one head of the dragon; two more spring up in its place."

I laughed and answered, "Especially in the beginning I was bound and determined to be Mrs. Martyr. Any old reason would do. And lots of my reasons had more to do with my convenience than my love for Bill. I couldn't open a jar, I couldn't get the car started, or I couldn't move a bureau to a new spot where I wanted to try it."

It isn't any one thing that you particularly mind," said another widow. "You feel deserted and unfairly treated by fate having nobody to help you with anything. You resent having the whole burden laid on your shoulders after so many years of having a partner to lift his end."

The topic of conversation veered, and I never had a chance to say that there was one thing that I particularly minded: my new role as Maintenance (Wo)Man. Before Bill's illness, he had assumed that was his role, so he took responsibility for every loose screw in the house. Then during his illness, though it was necessarily mine, I was so preoccupied that I didn't even notice that a paint job was needed here, a repair job there. I neglected the house, and if it had fallen down around my ears, I would hardly have raised an eyebrow. After Bill died, I did notice, and I missed (and miss) Bill's doing many odd jobs that I couldn't do.

Not that he was the handyman *par excellence*; he wasn't. But when he ran into a situation that needed attention, he would study it (stubborn as he was) as a scientist studies a problem in the lab, until he found a way to do something about it.

By contrast, I didn't know where to start. Most kindergarten dropouts know more about mechanical things than I do. Bill used to laugh and think my stupidity and ignorance "cute." In fact, he once joked, "Anything more mechanical than turning a doorknob baffles my favorite wife." I was such an ignoramus that when (right after Bill had the stroke) Joe asked, "Mother, where's the valve that controls the water to the outside faucet? With freezing weather ahead, it should be turned off," I answered, "We've lived in this house only twenty-one years, and I haven't the faintest idea."

Every year since (Joe having found it) I've turned it off, but I'm always afraid I'll forget it. I'm always afraid I'll forget other crucial jobs too, and if I do remember one, I'm afraid I'll botch it. Beyond changing a light bulb, I'll never touch anything to do with electricity because I'm convinced I'd blow the house up. And as for carpentry— well, the less said the better.

No doubt, I should tell myself: You're acting like a spoiled brat. It's never too late to learn, so get with it.

Maybe you've long since done that. It's the sensible thing to do. Or maybe you've never felt acutely sorry for yourself about this sort of thing because you're like the widow who told me, "I was always the one who first noticed something needed repair or replacing. I was always the one who hired the workmen too."

Another bugbear— hiring! It's always difficult even for the experienced person to get competent workmen; for the inexperienced it seems impossible. And the smaller the task the more impossible to get anyone at all, competent or incompetent. With dint of trying, you can get a roofer to roof the whole house, or a plumber to install a new hot water heater, but how can you get someone to take care of the pesky little jobs like fixing the spring on the back door screen, knocking down a hornet's nest on the porch, or putting a couple of new slats in the rose-arbor? Whom shall I get? Who will come— were questions I grappled with, often despairingly.

Moreover, now that I had to hire people to do jobs that Bill would routinely have taken care of, I was appalled at how much I had to pay them. I didn't know if the workmen were overcharging or not, and in many instances I didn't know if they were doing a good job or a bad.

When I complained about all this to another widow, she answered, "That's the main reason I sold my house and took an apartment. Many widows do."

Her words were a needed dash of cold water in my face. They made me realize that I too could move to an apartment, but I didn't want to. I preferred, even without Bill, to stay in the house. Since this was my own choice, I shouldn't feel sorry for myself and fuss about what the choice entailed. There's a Spanish proverb that translates roughly, "Get what you want from life but be willing to pay for it."

Another dousing with much-needed cold water came the day I happened to meet in close succession a severely handicapped youngish woman who (probably because of her handicap) had never married and the parents of a retarded boy. A message to me: *You* are feeling sorry for yourself? Where is your sense of proportion?

Self pity exited from center stage, but (wouldn't you know?) it stayed in the wings and has come back since for brief appearances.

And not only has it come back to make me feel sorry again that I'm Maintenance Man here at Coakley Manor but sorry about other aspects of my widowhood. Until Bill's stroke, he and I had a pattern for evenings at home: read, listen to the hi-fi or a TV program, and, above all, talk to each other. We were content with our pattern. After Bill died, I reverted to the reading, the hi-fi, and the TV, but the talk was lacking, and I was anything *but* content. Though I might not be consciously thinking about my bereavement, I found myself filled with a vague malaise that had me on edge and itchy.

Sometimes I simply couldn't manage to sit still and read or look at or listen to anything. Then I'd try solitaire or crossword puzzles.

When I mentioned my restlessness to another widow, she said, "I felt the same way. I resorted to knitting and needlepoint. They helped."

I can well understand the women who turn to liquor. It does ease jittery nerves and makes the self pity more bearable. When I realized how much I relied on a drink, or two, or three, I rationed myself to a drink before dinner and a nightcap. I was afraid I'd find myself with the bottle parked beside me all evening. It would be an easy out and to take it might mean, before I realized it, Wham-o, I'm an alcoholic.

Another widow told me "In the evenings, I would nibble away at candy, or I'd eat huge bowls of ice cream. I seemed to have this gnawing feeling that I had to satisfy. After a while I woke up to the fact that I was putting on weight. Now I have to half-starve myself to take it off. I wish somebody had told me early on: 'You're eating not because you're physically hungry; you're lonely and sorry for yourself, and you've regressed to the child who gets a lollipop to stop her tears.'"

In her book, *Heart Sounds*, Martha Lear talks about "the price" you have to pay for having once enjoyed intimacy, and she declares, "There is no way to have intimacy without dependency. You love, you need . . ."

Another widow (quoted by Michael A. Simpson, the British psychiatrist) talks about "the similarity between grief and a drug addict's withdrawal. I'd been infatuated by (addicted to) Kurt and stopped dead in my tracks was like going 'cold turkey.'"

Do you just have to endure the "withdrawal" jitters, or can you do anything to calm them?

Well, you don't have to be a *complete* loner, and contact with people helps. To begin with, you can use the phone. You can phone your married children or other relatives. I don't have one relative in Pennsylvania, but I could still phone long distance. I phoned (and phone) Jeanne and Joe, my sisters, my cousins. I don't go as far as Marie (who had four of her six children living out of state) when she said, "I'd rather go without indoor plumbing than a telephone," but I do think the phone is a marvelous instrument of comparatively cheap psychotherapy.

You don't want to overdo calls to relatives and wear out your welcome-by-wire so— "Elementary, my dear Watson"— you make other calls. You can call your friends, too— often another widow. You may make a date when you call to go to dinner the following evening. You never have any trouble finding a dinner partner among your widow friends; ninety-nine percent of them hate cooking for themselves alone and hate still more eating alone.

Now, if you say eating out is expensive, the only answer is: It surely is! But again, not as expensive as a psychiatrist's fee. And perhaps it tends to keep the cost down to go the way most widows want to go, "Dutch," or as Marie used to say, "No, not Dutch. Let's put it, 'I'll treat you and you treat me.'"

If you're inhibited about going out in the evening male-less, you'll get over it. I did and I belong to the generation that thought going out at night always called for a man. When I found out that I very seldom had a man available, I saw the alternative was to become a semirecluse. I didn't want that. I'll admit that I didn't begin to enjoy the company of my friends as I did the company of Bill, but because I couldn't have First Prize, it didn't seem sensible to spurn Second or Third Prize, and stay home with my own company which, in the mood I was in then, was at most Booby Prize.

Weekends and holidays had me in a dither longer than did weeknights. They are the Slough of Despond for widows, especially if you have no nearby children and grandchildren. You have to do the best you can with them, and if you plan ahead, surprisingly you can often find some little nuggets of fun. You can learn which of your friends is going to be in town for the Thanksgiving or the Fourth of July weekend and then arrange to do something with her. If you wait until the eleventh hour, often you can't even get reservations at a restaurant, much less at a resort where you might have enjoyed going for the weekend.

If you have no friends staying in town for that weekend, don't give up and resign yourself to loneliness. Though it wasn't very original, I hit on a way out of that dilemma. Faced with a bleak holiday or for that matter with any stretch of time when I was in the throes of restlessness, I'd ask myself: What can I do for somebody else? Then I'd get moving.

When I realized the formula pulled me out of the doldrums — or helped pull me out — I sat down and made a list of people I knew who had troubles or problems or illnesses. (It was amazing how long the list was.) It began with two elderly women. One was a nonegenarian, mother of a recently deceased writer-friend of mind. This poor lady could not get over her "child's" death. At least once in a while I took her (and still do take her) out for lunch. The other old lady is a trifle younger, but she can no longer drive, and her chief annoyance in life seems to be that she can't get out to buy a package of pins at Woolworth's or to the bank to draw a few dollars. Occasionally, I can and do chauffeur her.

Just phoning somebody or writing a short note to somebody who has troubles or illness is another ploy. You have to think at least briefly of her (or him) instead of yourself and your woes.

Many years ago I saw a movie in which the protagonist was shown what the world would have been like if he had never lived; it would have been much sadder. He had done all sorts of things to help other people, beginning with the great act of saving his brother from drowning. I couldn't do great acts, but I could do Boy Scout "good deeds" once in a while, and I hope they helped other people. They certainly helped, and help, me.

> If I can stop one heart from breaking,
> I shall not live in vain;
> If I can ease one life the aching,
> Or cool some pain,
> Or help one fainting robin
> Onto his nest again,
> I shall not live in vain.

EMILY DICKINSON

21

"Contentment is a form of courage."
Whoever said that must have understood the struggles of a widow. When you have reached contentment, you have reached the ultimate state, a notch above mere acceptance.

I remember saying to a widow friend, "A widow is like a man who has lost an arm. He misses it but he learns to manage somehow with just the one he has left. Eventually he even enjoys life again."

Acceptance comes then when you learn to live with the situation; contentment when you begin to enjoy life again.

My first feeling of contentment came one summer night about sixteen months after Bill died. It seemed that a soft serenity enveloped me. (I don't mean a glowing happiness, but I repeat a serenity— and yes, a contentment.) I had gone with friends to a symphony concert held in a semi-open-air theatre in the park. The setting was idyllic, and the music, which included selections from a Missa Solemnis, was so awe evoking that I felt wafted upward toward the farthest star in the sky.

Then the thought struck me: If I have to live without Bill, I have as good and as smooth a life as I can reasonably hope for. I didn't make a neat count of my blessings, but my mind took a panoramic sweep of my loving family and friends, my modestly comfortable financial set up, my absorbing profession, and the rest. But above all, I was conscious of something colossal. Although I did not have Bill physically beside me, I was positive at that instant he was looking after me. I had his love and protection. I not only believed, I *felt* just then the truth of the words, "Those who die in grace are no farther than God, and God is very near."

My euphoria faded and has never returned with quite the same beautiful balm. Yet I have found other moments of contentment — and oddly enough they've often come during moments of solitude. Solitude no longer appalls me for now I know that to be alone is not necessarily to be lonely. In fact, I think I can say truthfully that I am reasonably content, not just for moments, but that contentment is now my prevailing state of mind. Someone has said that "After sorrow comes maturation, and after maturation comes fruit." The fruit is, I think, a kind of contentment.

You can't hurry the process of reaching contentment by wishing on a star. For the most part it grows naturally, but you would probably stunt, if not stop, the growth if you did not at the same time make some efforts to fashion for yourself a new life.

You may do it through remarriage. It seems that if you have no children at home and you remarry, you usually do so within the first year of widowhood. During that year, you often feel that you cannot survive alone. Afterwards, if you don't remarry, you find out that you can survive, and you become perhaps a little selfish because you begin to prize your complete independence and the lifestyle that doesn't ask you to consider anybody else's happiness or convenience. You're unwilling to give any of that up unless the man were a paragon — and then some.

Many widows of course have no opportunity to remarry.

Others, goaded by loneliness, eagerly grab the first opportunity that comes along, and perhaps end up with a man totally unsuitable or one who wants to sponge on them.

Still others don't see their opportunities, for as one widow put it, "If you want to remarry, you have to act like a poker player and declare yourself in the game."

Obviously, remarriage is something to weigh carefully.

A few widows might agree with the woman who told me, "Remarriage would be disloyalty to Ed," but I answered her, "Remarriage takes nothing from Ed, and perhaps it just proves your ability to stretch your heart to make room for another love."

For myself I've never been sure that I have the ability nor the time left in my lifespan for remarriage. I'm a veteran of thirty-six years of matrimony with Bill. In the unlikely event that anybody whose proposal seemed tempting to me wanted to marry me, I think I'd say, "After that many years of shared experiences and shared private jokes that themselves took years in the building, there wouldn't be time nor, on my part, the inclination to throw myself wholeheartedly into the duplication of such a union."

On second thought, "duplication" is of course the wrong word. You never really duplicate an interpersonal attachment. You can try to fashion something fine in *another* way for each is unique.

Now, if you don't remarry, you still have to build a new life or at least enter a new phase of the old life.

I was blessed that I had my writing. During the second year I took steps to return to that in a more serious way than writing occasional, when-I-felt-like-it, free-lance articles. I researched a subject, planning to write a book about it, then approached a number of publishers with my idea. Although one publisher offered me a contract and an advance, I never wrote that particular book; I had just contracted to write another book which an editor who had edited previous books of mine asked me to write.[1]

His choice of subject would not have been mine, but the absorbing work was welcome.

Absorbing and creative work is certainly an important plank in the platform of contentment. It can be of various sorts. Coming home from Sea Island, Georgia, recently I fell into conversation with a retired school teacher of perhaps seventy who said she had just taken up oilpainting and loved it. "It opens up a whole new world," she said.

So never too old! Grandma Moses *began* painting at age seventy-eight.

But work, no matter how absorbing or creative, doesn't take the place of love. If you have children and grandchildren, that helps mightily and is, in most cases, another plank.

Is something still lacking?

If there is still a void, what is the ultimate solution?

Certainly you can't achieve the ultimate contentment by the determination and willpower that makes you grit your teeth and say, "Damn it, I'll be content if it kills me." You can achieve it by the willpower that means you are willing to put your life in God's hands. As Augustine said, "Our hearts are restless until they rest in Thee, oh God."

When I realized this, I saw that I should at least make an effort, even if I never quite succeeded, to turn to God and ask Him to make my maimed life whole once more through His love.

C.S. Lewis wrote in his book, *The Four Loves,* that "the very purpose of bereavement . . . may be to compel us to believe, what we cannot feel, that God is our true Beloved."

The idea put that way sounds very exalted and rather frightening, but I remembered that my sister who is a nun said something similar, something about God being able to more than take the place of any human love.

I certainly didn't argue with her because it is obvious that the Being Who is Himself Love could take the place of the best of husbands *if* a person could only open her heart to Him.

"Ay, there's the rub," Sister— to open your heart to Him.

Often I felt that I couldn't even pray. It was then that I turned to the Blessed Mother and asked her to be my proxy, my surrogate, my stand-in, and pray in my stead. Meaning the words in exactly that sense, I repeated the familiar plea of the Hail Mary, "Pray for us sinners." Often, too, when I felt anything but prayerful, I'd pick up a spiritual book. St. Teresa of Avila said she seldom attempted to pray without first reading a spiritual book.

Still it's hard to feel that you really love God, so it was encouraging to me to come across a spiritual writer who advised, "If thou thinkest that thou canst not love, then desire to love; if thou canst not even do this, then pray for the desire to love." Also I was encouraged by St. Philip Neri who purportedly prayed, "Oh Lord help. I don't love You at all." In fact, I used Philip's prayer and I pled with God, "Dear Lord, every life story should be a love story. Make mine that to the end."

Even so, I figured that since the love of God is bound up with the love of neighbor, you could begin with the less exalted love of your fellowman. Love of neighbor in the moral sense, thank Heaven, doesn't mean you have to feel attraction toward or affection for him. It means you have to desire his wellbeing and rise to the occasion when a Good Samaritan-like opportunity comes along.

That much I can do, can't I?, I asked myself.

I realized then that I had been trying to do something kind for other people fairly often. That hardly qualified as unselfish, religious love of neighbor since my motive had been mostly to distract myself from my sorrow. Now the trick was to substitute the better motive.

When I tried to do that, I found out that love goes in circles. The more you love your neighbor who is God's child, the more you love God, and the more you love God, the more you love your neighbor. The reason is of course that your neighbor, in the "least brethren" sense, *is* God. ("As long as you did it to one of these my least brethren, you did it unto me."[2]) It's like the old Christopher legend or fantasy. St. Christopher was the neo-Hercules who used to act as a human ferry by carrying travelers on his back across a turbulent stream. One day a little boy whom he was carrying suddenly seemed to grow unbearably heavy in midstream. Looking up, Christopher saw that the boy was aureated in light: He was the Christ Child.

Who feels like bothering with bores or other unattractive people, so to follow the kindness program you need to hang onto the "least brethren" text and the Christopher legend. Then if you ever come to the point where you glimpse God in other people, you'll know He is close — and that He is in you too.

Thinking about that I remembered the words Buzz Aldrin

had in his kit when he went to the moon in July 1969, and they took on new meaning:

> The light of God surrounds me
> The love of God enfolds me
> The power of God protects me
> The presence of God watches over me.
> Wherever I am, God is.

To grasp those words *fully* must surely mean to have one foot in Heaven already. A Carmelite nun wrote, "I have found Heaven on earth for Heaven is God, and God is in my soul. On the day that I realized this, I saw all things in a new light."

You and I may not have found our "Heaven on earth" yet. I know I haven't. Yet I am convinced that awareness of God's presence, even though it be vague and intermittent, increases love and hence contentment. You know by faith, if not by feeling, that you have an invisible Companion and Friend. And if His presence at first gives you no joy, I don't see any answer but to keep on trying to heighten the awareness. *Instant* love of God and neighbor isn't on the market; only instant coffee is.

John McKee wrote in *The Enemy Within the Gates,* about the legendary lay brother, nicknamed "The Smiler." Asked why he always smiled, the brother replied, "Because no man can take my God from me."

When I was gathering material for my book about television, I had to spend endless hours watching show after show, and I didn't always enjoy my occupation; at the same time though, because of sheer loneliness, I took some solace in hearing a human voice in the house. Actually, I could have said to myself: You can always tune in to the voice of the Friend, Who abides in the depths of your soul. There is, but there should *not* be, such a thing as a lonely believer.

In a surprising place, I found a motto that I hoped someday I could sincerely adopt. Often in a newspaper, I'd see a jewelry store ad for a gold pendant engraved with the words, "Je t'aime plus qu'hier, moins que demain." (I love you more than [I did] yesterday, less than [I will] tomorrow.) Wouldn't it be great if I could say that about my love of God? I couldn't, and I can't.

But it seems logical that love, which is spiritual wealth or grace, should eventually increase according to the rules for increasing material wealth. If you amass a small capital, it becomes easier from then on to make money, for as the saying goes, "It takes money to make money." So if you gain a little heap of graces, you can build on that and get more grace. The difference between the material and the spiritual is that the latter has no end, for God's grace is limitless.

So my dictum to myself was: Move toward love— or better said, move toward God Who is love. He alone brings wholeness.

Many people say that Transcendental Meditation helps them, and they repeat a nondefinable word or "Mantra." I tried instead spending a few minutes repeating over and over the word, "Jesus" or "God." Sometimes I used my rosary, a bead for each repetition, and let myself all the while bask, as it were, in the light of His presence. It seemed, and seems, to help.

The love which *is* God brings comfort, for comfort is not exactly ease; it is strength. The word itself is a combination of the Latin "con," meaning "with" and "fortare," meaning "to strengthen," so it literally means to have what it takes to be strengthened. If you are comforted, you have strength enough to bear whatever you must bear because an omnipotent God bears it with you.

Then love brings gratitude. I had told myself earlier that I should be grateful to God for giving me a good marriage with Bill. Now, I thought I should also be grateful to God for being with me. In fact, since I wanted to show that God helped me through Bill's illness, and death, and that He is helping me through widowhood, it was gratitude that sparked this book.

My story is a neo-version of the old story about the man who was walking along the beach with the Lord. Looking back, the man saw the events of the past, and with the events there were two sets of footprints, one his, the other the Lord's. Then he took a second look, and he noticed that through the very saddest and roughest events of his life, there ran only one set of foot-prints. "Why?" he asked the Lord. "Why weren't You with me at the worse moments of my life?"

The Lord answered, "I was. During the worst moments I car-ried you."

No, I was not, and I am not alone. I never will be.

Neither are you, for the "The Lord is nigh.[3]"

✢ Notes

Chapter 1
1. Ps. 123:8

Chapter 2
1. Mt. 27:46
2. Gen. 18:14
3. Jn. 2:3,5
4. Mk. 9:23

Chapter 4
1. Ps. 117:16, 17

Chapter 5
1. Lk. 1:30, 31
2. Jean Baptiste Lacordaire (1802-1861) was a famous and controversial pulpit orator who took France by storm in the nineteenth century.
3. Acts 5:15
4. Lk. 11:9

Chapter 6
1. Ps. 144:1

Chapter 7
1. Mk. 9:23
2. Jn. 6:69
3. Mt. 26:39
4. Jn. 6:56
5. Lk. 1:42, 44
6. Jn. 14:2
7. Mk. 10:51
8. Samuel Hoffenstein, XVIII, "Year In, You're Out," *The Complete Poetry of Samuel Hoffenstein* (New York: Random House, Modern Library, 1954).
9. Ps. 33:20
10. Ps. 17:19, 20

Chapter 8
1. Gal. 2:20
2. Ps. 88:2

Chapter 9
1. Mt. 6:33
2. Jas. 5:7
3. Jn. 15:5

Chapter 10
1. Ps. 3:5
2. Is. 38:5
3. Mt. 8:13
4. Mt. 15:27
5. Job 26:2

Chapter 11
1. 2 Kg. 22;6
2. Ps. 123:8

Chapter 12
1. Mt. 7:7
2. Mt. 6:34

Chapter 14
1. Ps.9:10
2. Jer. 15:20
3. Charles L. O'Donnell, *A Rhyme of the Road and Other Poems* (London Longmans Green, 1928).
4. Lk.20:37
5. 1 Th. 4:12-15
6. Wisd. 3:1-5:16; Dan. 12:2; Job 19:25, 26; Mt. 5:12, 19:29, 22:31, 32, 25:46; Lk. 14:14, 18:30; Jn. 3:16, 5:21, 24 6:40, 50, 52, 55, 59, 69; Acts 13:46, 24:15; Rom. 6:22, 23; Gal. 6:8; 2 Cor. 5:1; 1 Tim. 1:16; 2 Tim. 2:10; 1 Jn. 1:2

Chapter 15
1. 1 Cor. 13:3, 1
2. 2 Macc. 12:46
3. Lk. 1:38

Chapter 16
1. Lynn Caine, *Widow* (New York: William Morrow, 1974).

184

Chapter 18
1. If you have any trouble deciding what to do, or need other advice you might write to: AARP Widowed Persons Service
                        1909 K Street N.W.
                        Washington, D.C.20049
   This organization will supply information about programs in your area.
      Or write to: Parents Without Partners which has branches in various places, including California, New York, and Washington, D.C.
      Or write to: To Live Again
   This organization has branches in Philadelphia, Wilmington, and a few other places.

Chapter 19
1. Is. 48:22
2. Mt. 25:13
3. Mt. 6:20
4. 1 Pe. 5:7
5. Ps. 22:4

Chapter 20
1. Emily Dickinson, *Selected Poems of Emily Dickinson* (New York: Modern Library, 1924).

Chapter 21
1. Mary Lewis Coakley, *The Moral Case Against TV* (New Rochelle, N.Y.: Arlington House, 1977).
2. Mt. 25:40
3. Ps. 33:19

⚜ References

Isaac Asimov, *The Human Brain*. Boston: Houghton Mifflin, 1963.

Lynn Caine, *Widow*. New York: Morrow, 1974.

Lewis Carroll, *Alice's Adventures in Wonderland* and *Through the Looking Glass*. New York: Three Sirens Press.

Mary Lewis Coakley, *Never Date Women*. Milwaukee: The Bruce Publishing Co., 1964.

Mary Lewis Coakley, *Rated X: The Moral Case Against TV*. Arlington House Publishers, 1977.

Emily Dickinson, *Selected Poems of Emily Dickinson*. New York: Modern Library, 1924.

Martha Weinman Lear, *Heart Sounds*. New York: Simon & Shuster, 1980.

Sister Elizabeth of the Trinity, *The Praise of Glory*. Maryland: Newman Press, 1962.

Walter Farrell, O.P., S.T.M. and Martin J. Healy S.T.D., *My Way of Life: Pocket Edition of St. Thomas*. New York: Confraternity of the Precious Blood, 1952.

Edmund Fuller, *Thesaurus of Epigrams*. New York: Garden City Publishing Co., Inc., 1948

Samuel Hoffenstein, *The Complete Poetry of Samuel Hoffenstein*. New York: Modern Library, 1954.

Thomas à Kempis, *The Imitation of Christ*. New York: Hurst & Co., The Companion Books.

Elizabeth Kübler-Ross, *Questions and Answers on Death and Dying*. New York: Macmillan, 1972.

Bernadine Kreis and Alice Pattie, *Up From Grief*. New York: Seabury Press, 1969.

C. S. Lewis, *The Four Loves*. New York: Harcourt, 1960.

C. S. Lewis, *A Grief Observed*. New York: Seabury Press, 1961.

Ruth Jean Lowensohn, *Survival Handbook for Widows*. Chicago: Follett, 1979.

Carson McCullers, *A Member of the Wedding*. New Directions Paperbacks, 1951.

Charles L. O'Donnell, *A Rhyme of the Road and Other Poems*

Isabella Tanes, *Love Must Not Be Wasted*. Crowell, New York, 1974.

Alfred Lord Tennyson, *The Poetic and Dramatic Works of Alfred Lord Tennyson*. Boston & New York: Houghton Mifflin Co., and The Riverside Press, Cambridge, 1889.